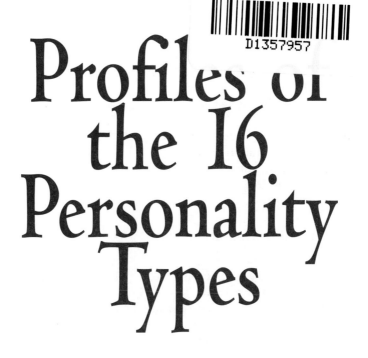

Profiles of the 16 Personality Types

By William C. Jeffries

The Author of

True to Type

*Taming the Scorpion:Preparing Business
for the Third Millennium*

Hannibal, Hummers & Hot Air Balloons

TM

**Buttermilk
Ridge
Publishing**

Published by:
Buttermilk Ridge Publishing
136 S. 9th Street, Ste. 18
Noblesville, IN 46060
www.buttermilkridgepublishing.com

Distributed by:
Executive Strategies International, Inc.
9620 Irishman's Run Lane
Zionsville, Indiana 46077
www.execustrat.com

Library of Congress Control Number 2002111914

Jeffries, William C.
    Profiles of the 16 Personality Types / William C. Jeffries
        p.   cm.
    ISBN 0-9723961-0-1

Back cover photo by Jennifer Marshall, MG Photography.

Printed in the USA

Table of Contents

Foreword

I have avoided writing profiles for the sixteen types for over a decade. I must admit that it is a daunting task. Even having worked with type for close to two decades, I find it almost presumptuous to try to understand all sixteen types thoroughly enough to commit my thoughts to paper. As I have read other authors' attempts over the years to capture the nuances of different personalities and styles, I have been appreciative of their efforts, but always found inconsistencies or biases in some of the portraits they published.

I am sometimes reluctant to hand out profiles to clients because some of them can strike participants as being as perfunctory and boilerplate as a newspaper's daily description of the twelve signs of the Zodiac. Indeed, some of the profiles I have read are just as generic and indiscriminate. Some strike me as being comprised of eight paragraphs on the eight preferences that are merely cut and pasted to sound like the sixteen types.

What I have attempted to do is to make each profile unique and idiosyncratic. There are twelve elements common to each profile:

- Four Letter Type and four Key Words
- Tag line
- Overview
- Other High Performers who share your type
- Snapshot
- Leadership Style
- Words to Live By
- Jobs and Careers that Attract Your Type

- Extended Profile
- Type and Age
- Type Under Stress
- Your Type and Ethics

There are also two places where you can take notes on other words you use to describe yourself and other people you know who share your personality type. It is my hope that you will use the profiles as a starting point for extended self-knowledge. As you read the profiles, read them with a pen or pencil in your hand. When you find parts of the suggested profile(s) that you do not believe are true of you, cross it out or put a check next to it. The idea is to personalize the profile to your life and see to what extent it rings true for you.

After you personalize it, however, please be willing to take the next step. The next step is, after you have marked up your profile indicating all those places where the profile does not match your view of yourself, to show it to someone who knows you very well and ask that person to read it. Don't be surprised if in several places where you crossed out a section claiming it was nothing like you, somebody else says "Oh, yes you do!" But that is the beginning of growth. To some extent our personalities are a combination of how we see ourselves and how others see us.

While the observation of thousands of people have gone into each of the profiles, they are intended to be descriptive not prescriptive. I hope they get clearer and better refined with each edition of this book.

If you have suggestions, criticisms, or comments about the profiles, please let me know. I will look forward to hearing from you. You can always reach me through our website at www.execustrat.com. If you would like to e-mail me directly, contact me at esipres6@earthlink.net or Bill.Jeffries@execustrat.com. If the old technology makes you feel better, you can always reach me on the POTS at (800) 977-1688.

ISTJ
Planner, Responsible, Trustee, Inspector
Mr., Mrs., or Ms. Responsibility

Overview: You have indicated that you prefer Introversion, Sensing, Thinking, and Judging as your favorite ways of dealing with the world around you. By selecting those preferences you join about 6% of the world's population who share the same personality type.

Other High Performers who share your type include: George Washington, Shaquille O'Neal (# 34, L. A. Lakers), Henry Ford, General Erwin Rommel (The Desert Fox), Attorney General John Ashcroft, Secretary of State James Baker, Governor Christy Todd Whitman, General Montgomery, Calvin Coolidge, Mariano Rivera (# 42, NY Yankees), and one third of all those persons in the military.

Snapshot: You are hard working, thorough, careful with details, and painstakingly systematic in your approach to life. Doing the right thing for the right reason and taking responsibility for your actions is the hallmark of your personality.

Leadership Style: Your type is one of the four most likely to rise to the top of large and complex organizations. In Fortune 500 Companies, your type comprises about 2.8 % of the presidents and CEO's, 29.5 % of senior and executive vice presidents, and 23.9 % of middle managers. For you, responsibility and organization are the bottom line. You prefer hierarchal organizations with a keen sense of tradition and a clearly articulated progression plan that includes specific roles and responsibilities. Position conveys responsibility. Saluting the rank, not the person, may have been first articulated by you, because it is the position that conveys authority. You prefer to take charge and reward others for responsible, consistent performance. After all, they are the traits you also value in yourself.

How many of these traits apply to you?

__ You are known for steady, reliable performance

__ You manage details with care and precision

__ You expect the right equipment at the right place at the right time

__ Working within the organizational structure is satisfying

__ If you make a commitment, you will honor it and follow through

__ If assigned a task, you will take charge firmly

__ You will follow the rules and reward others for doing so as well

__ You believe the organization you work for should provide job security and benefits

__ You prefer a sense of privacy to complete your assigned tasks

__ You expect those who report to you to be hard working and responsible

Words To Live By: reliable, painstaking, dependable, practical, sensible, duty bound, factual, truthful, organized, realistic, thorough, steadfast, and systematic.

Jobs and Careers that Attract Your Type: Military, business management, law enforcement, real estate, engineering (mechanical, electrical, aeronautical), law, finance and accounting, word processing, government agencies, regulatory compliance, corrections, sales, tax and estate planning, education administration, geology, meteorology, agriculture, aviation, the ministry, medicine, and pharmacology.

Words You Use to Describe Yourself: _____

Extended Profile: As one of the most practical of the six-teen types, you are the backbone of every organization you work with and the Rock of Gibraltar for your friends. You are thoroughly grounded in the present and can't be swayed by frivolous concerns. Novel ideas can seem flighty to you. You prefer a tried and true method for dealing with projects and jobs you are assigned. Visions have never impressed you. What does, is hard work, dedication, doing your duty, and being responsible.

Whether at work or at home, you prefer clear-cut roles and responsibilities. You tend to be conventional in your views of finances, gender, church, schools, and politics. The more predictable your environment is, the more you like it. You probably coined the phrase, "my home is my castle." It is the place where you can celebrate all those important rites, holidays, and traditions that your family uses to connect with its past. You fill it with useful posses-sions, nothing frivolous, but solid, well-made, practical furniture and appliances.

You have a splendid ability to deal with large amounts of data, without feeling overwhelmed, and are known for being precise and exacting in your work. And, you do not mind working for long periods of time without a break or the need for social intercourse. This skill comes so easily to you that you may not realize how exceptional you are. You may in fact underestimate your ability on a routine basis. You take pride in your ability to work hard and long, and prefer a solitary, quiet working place to do your best work. If the doorbell never rings and the telephone rests quietly in its cradle, you are just pleased.

Right and wrong, and good and bad are genuine categories

for you. You hold yourself accountable to the rules regarding these absolute categories and hold others accountable, as well. Your word is your bond. When you shake hands, the deal is done. Hence, you find the words "should" and "ought" helpful to clue others in to their responsibilities, as well. Justice is more important to you than mercy.

Because you are super dependable, you will tend to "join" organizations, not just attend functions. You do not attend church or synagogue, you join it. You do not just attend PTA meetings, you join the PTA. You coach little league soccer, collect money for the Heart Fund, join the Rotary, the Elks, the Masons, the Jaycees, and organize the neighborhood barbecue. You probably hold it in your backyard, because that is what a good citizen should do. And, of course, you vote! That is what a responsible citizen does.

You believe in country and probably God. Motherhood, apple pie, and a hot lunch for orphans are tenants of a solid life. Children should obey their parents, citizens should remove their hats during the national anthem, marriages should last more than five years, and the family dog should fetch the newspaper.

Type and Age: Although you have elected just four preferences as your "type," life is an ongoing experience of learning how to use all eight preferences at the appropriate time, for the appropriate task. You will develop different preferences at specific, predictable times in your life.

For your type, the flow is as follows:
Dominant—introverted Sensing (ages 8-15)
Auxiliary—extraverted Thinking (ages 16-30)
Tertiary—introverted Feeling (ages 31-40)
Inferior—extraverted iNtuition (ages 41-55)

What we refer to as your Dominant function is Sensing, which you express internally. To do your best work, you need quiet, alone time to gather data, perform the assay, and understand what information is necessary to help you. You probably developed this function first, between the ages 8-15. When you judge and analyze the data, you use your Auxiliary function, which is Thinking judgment. This function is expressed in the outer world; hence, you extravert it. This function was likely developed from the ages of 16-30. Hence, by the end of college or beginning of your early professional years, the sensing–thinking ground floor to your personality has been laid. The middle two letters of your personality type become the team of preferences that you will trust the most into the beginning of midlife.

About the age of 31, one of your non-preferences asks to be dealt with. We call it your Tertiary function. For your type, it is Feeling judgment, which you introvert. Your best decision making, relative to personal, value-related concerns, will be done alone, in the internal world. Others may not know you are reflecting on such concerns, but they will be very important to you. From the ages of 31 to about 40 you will develop this capacity to empathize. Your type does not change, but you learn how to use this non-preference when required. Your last preference to be developed we call the Inferior function. For you, it is iNtuition, which you extravert. Between the ages of 41-55, you will become more comfortable trading in the external world of ideas, concepts, and possibilities.

Type, then, is far more than just 4 letters on a report form. If all goes well, and it rarely does, by late midlife, you will have developed the capacity to use each of the 8 preferences when needed, with some degree of sophistication. We call this process the full development of type.

Type under Stress: Under severe stress, your normally rational type becomes obsessed with irrelevancies and overly pessimistic. Normally, when using your dominant introverted Sensing function, you are good at keeping track of essentials and being realistic in your approach to problems. When you suddenly get trapped working out of your inferior function, which is extraverted iNtuition, everything changes. You believe you are cornered and can't see a way out. You get stuck in a rut and can't see the forest for the trees. Attending to any relevant data will become a major chore. Pessimism will attend everything you do and say, and you will fear the future and its consequences in purely negative ways. When you do act, it may be spontaneously and without forethought. Buying that new car without consulting *Consumer Reports* becomes a real possibility. Doing something irresponsible and reveling in it might just excite you.

Your Type and Ethics: Your type is one of four, for whom values are crystal clear. If someone wants to know what is right or wrong, you can find it written down somewhere, in black and white. You will gladly take us to volume III, page 26 and show us rules one through fifteen. You will follow them. We should too. The rules have the status of laws, and ethical people should be expected to agree upon their meaning and follow them. You are quite suspicious of those who might flaunt the rules and see such individuals as reckless. Likewise, those who might want to decide differently, depending on the situation, strike you as flaky and irresponsible. You have little sympathy for those who violate the established values and want to have them punished for their transgressions. The rules are there for our mutual good, and a mood of righteous indignation often pervades your sense of required justice.

Other ISTJ's who you know: _____

ISFJ
Dutiful, Supporter, Conservator, Protector
The Power Behind the Throne

Overview: You have indicated that you prefer Introversion, Sensing, Feeling, and Judging as your favorite ways of dealing with the world around you. By selecting those preferences, you join about 6% of the world's population who share the same personality type.

Other High Performers who share your type include: Nancy Reagan, George Bush (41), General Omar Bradley, Reggie White, Laura Bush, Johnny Carson, Jimmy Carter, and Radar O'Reilly. This is also the modal type (regardless of gender) for spouses and partners of military members and business managers.

Snapshot: You are a considerate and kind person who can easily sympathize with others. If someone is in need, you are willing to go to any lengths to assist them. Your style is to be the unassuming power behind the throne.

Leadership Style: As your type moves up in the organization, you do so quietly in a value-centered way—without seeking acclaim or notoriety. In Fortune 500 Companies, your type comprises less than 1 % of presidents and CEO's, about 1.7 % of the senior and executive vice presidents, and 4.7 % of middle managers. Your colleagues know that you are extraordinarily dependable, and that you will follow through with commitments you make to your organization and customers alike. Your loyalty, on which you pride yourself, is directed to people, not the organization. While you place a high value on service, it is often service you perform behind the scenes.

How many of these traits apply to you?

__ Following the rules and observing conventional behaviors is appealing to you

__ You work behind the scenes to influence the results

__ Working within a hierarchy is a comfortable role

__ You expect both yourself and others to comply with the organization's needs and expectations

__ You will follow through and expect others to do so as well

__ You are painstaking in your approach to details

__ You willingly expend effort to assist others

__ The right things in the right place make you a happy person

__ Having clear organizational goals helps you to do your job

__ Duty and personal commitments are high on your list of core values

Words to Live By: responsible, meticulous, patient, organized, helpful, detailed, protective, conscientious, devoted, traditional, practical, loyal, and service-oriented.

Jobs and Careers That Attract Your Type: Engineering (mining and electrical), health care (family physician, dietician, therapist, optician, radiologist, RN's, LPN's) veterinarian, elementary school teacher, human resources, librarian, probation officers, guidance counselors, special education, alcohol and drug counselor, secretary, clergy, credit counselor, accountant, interior decorator, government administrator, musician, artist, customer service specialist, real estate agent, inn keeper, bed and breakfast manager, benefits administrator, and consultant.

Words You Use to Describe Yourself:_____

Extended Profile: As one of the most realistic of the sixteen types, you prefer to live your life in a simple, practical, and unassuming way. You are patient with routine tasks and do not mind being the one to do the common tasks necessary to accomplish a job. As the "power behind the throne," others often are unaware of the power you have to influence events and people. You have no need to assert that moral authority. You just act upon it responsibly.

When you are in jobs that require accuracy and attention to detail, you can be counted on to perform your work with precision and care. When working with others who are not as attentive to detail, you may see them as unreliable, at best. You wouldn't be so "careless," and neither should they. In fact the words "should" and "ought" are two words that others tend to associate with you.

You are not one to rush into tasks or relationships frivolously. You take your time understanding requirements and motives—something you are very good at, by the way. You prefer receiving an assignment where the tasks, roles, outcomes, and responsibilities are all spelled out very clearly. Broad, sweeping assignments such as, act as project manager for the implementation of SAP, open new markets to Asia, or eliminate the Taliban in Afghanistan normally do not appeal to you.

What the organization has done in the past, family traditions your grandparents brought to this country from Europe, and core values you learned at the knee of parents, rabbis, Sunday school teachers, and high school coaches are very important to you. Again, these are things we "should" do. There are clear-cut rights and clear-cut wrongs, and wise people should pay attention to the differences.

Children should be seen and not heard. Families should

have two parents—one male and one female. Trick or treaters at Halloween should wear masks and costumes or you shouldn't be expected to put anything in their bags. Schools should teach the Constitution and the Bill of Rights, and children should say the Pledge of Allegiance in school every day, including the phrase, "in God we trust"! The Boy Scouts and Girl Scouts of America are good and wholesome, and if one of them shows up at your front door wearing a uniform, you should buy what they are selling. And, when the flag passes by, you should stand up and put your right hand over your heart. Patriotism is a traditional value, and it is good.

Both at home and at work, you tend to be financially conservative. You will approve a reasonable budget, no more, no less, and hold employees accountable for working within its limits. Over spending is irresponsible. When you purchase materials, you will give your employees just the supplies they need. Waste strikes you as reckless and probably immoral.

At home, you may save so much for the future that you skimp on the present. Taking care of your family's financial future is a responsible thing to do. You believe you should not run up high debt on your credit cards; indeed, if you do let that happen, you are probably under extraordinary stress. Being a traditionalist, you value a simple life. When you purchase furniture, it is probably good quality but designed to last a lifetime, and, it comes with a money back guarantee.

You take pleasure in feeling useful to others and often go out of the way to help others and to take on responsibilities that, quite frankly, are not yours. You may even try to bail out others who have problems with debt, alcohol, drugs, or gambling, and have to take care not to become codependent with others with dysfunctional behaviors.

You have probably made Murphy's law a key tenet of your approach to life. In your outlook on the market, your fiscal responsibility, and your concern for relationships, a certain air of pessimism seems warranted.

Overall, your life is impacted by a serious work ethic. Work comes first, play later; indeed, you probably believe that one has to earn his or her right to play. This attitude even pervades your free time, and leisure time probably includes doing projects that need to be completed. A real vacation, lounging on the beach, or snow boarding for hours probably makes you feel guilty. You would rather power wash the deck, clean the pool, transplant shrubs, change the oil in the car, or weed whack those weeds taking over the hammock in the back yard. By golly, that's fun!

Type and Age: Although you have elected just four preferences as your "type," life is an ongoing experience of learning how to use all eight preferences at the appropriate time, for the appropriate task. You will develop different preferences at specific, predictable times in your life.

For your type, the flow is as follows:
    Dominant—introverted Sensing (ages 8-15)
    Auxiliary—extraverted Feeling (ages 16-30)
    Tertiary—introverted Thinking (ages 31-40)
    Inferior—extraverted iNtuition (ages 41-55)

What we refer to as your Dominant function, is Sensing, which you express internally. To do your best work, you need quiet, alone time to gather data, perform the assay, and understand what information is necessary to help you. You probably developed this function first, between the ages 8-15. When you judge and come to closure on the data, you use your Auxiliary function, which is Feeling judgment. This function is expressed in the outer world; hence, you extravert it. This function was likely developed between the ages of 16-30. Hence, by the end of college or the beginning of your early professional years, the Sensing–Feeling ground floor to your personality has been laid. The middle two letters of your personality type become the team of preferences that you will trust the most into the beginning of midlife.

About the age of 31, one of your non-preferences asks to be dealt with. We call it your Tertiary function. For your type, it is Thinking judgment, which you introvert. Your best analysis when you exercise cause and effect reasoning will be done alone, in the internal world. Others may not know you are judging analytically, but the process begins to be important to you. From the ages of 31 to about 40, you will develop this analytical interest. Your type does not change, but you learn how to use this non-preference when required. Your last preference to be developed we call the Inferior function. For you, it is iNtuition, which you extravert. Between the ages of 41-55, you will become more comfortable trading in the external world of ideas and possibilities.

Type, then, is far more than just 4 letters on a report form. If all goes well, and it rarely does, by late midlife, you will have developed the capacity to use each of the 8 prefer-ences when needed, with some degree of sophistication. We call this process the full development of type.

Type Under Stress: Under heavy stress, your normally supportive style becomes overly pessimistic. Normally, when using your dominant introverted Sensing function you do a great job recognizing what needs to be done, and you recognize the pertinent facts and dismiss the rest. When you suddenly get trapped working out of your inferior function, which is extraverted iNtuition, everything changes. Your thoughts about the future all become negative and accompanied by fear and trepidation. The daughter due home at 10 pm is lying in a wreck injured from a car accident; the report that is late, includes negative comments about your division, and the author is afraid to show it to you; the commotion on the first floor is the 60 Minutes News Team coming to interview you about the rash of safety violations at your main plant; and that creak in the hall stairwell, is Jason making his scary return to your second floor bedroom. You feel trapped in a rut and can't see a way out. Pessimism attends your every comment. Life isn't fun.

Your Type and Ethics: Your type is one of four, for whom values are crystal clear. If someone wants to know what is right or wrong, you can find it written down somewhere, in black and white. You will gladly take us to volume III, page 26 and show us rules one through fifteen. You will follow them. We should too. The rules have the status of laws, and ethical people should be expected to agree upon their meaning and follow them. You are quite suspicious of those who might flaunt the rules and see such individuals as reckless. Likewise, those who might want to decide differently, depending on the situation, strike you as flaky and irresponsible. You have little sympathy for those who violate the established values and want to have them punished for their transgressions. The rules are there for our mutual good, and a mood of righteous indignation often pervades your sense of required justice.

Other ISFJ's who you know:_____

INFJ
Developer, Inspirer, Author, Foreseer
Value-Centered Change Agent

Overview: You have indicated that you prefer Introversion, iNtuition, Feeling, and Judging as your favorite ways of dealing with the world around you. By selecting those preferences, you join about 1% of the world's population who share the same personality type.

Other High Performers who share your type include: General Robert E. Lee, Thomas Jefferson, Mother Teresa, Sigmund Freud, Katharine Briggs, and Jesus of Nazareth.

Snapshot: Your style is to assert your influence quietly and compassionately, with genuine trust in your vision for life. Maintaining harmony is very important to you in your business, family, and dealings with others.

Leadership Style: In Fortune 500 Companies, your type comprises less than 1 % of presidents and CEO's, 1 % of senior and executive vice presidents and 1.5 % of middle managers. You place great trust in your own vision and are often an inspiration to others because of your value-centered approach to living up to it. Your strong desire to contribute to the welfare of others helps you to win others' cooperation, without having to demand it. Once you know what succeeding looks like, you will exert personal energy almost endlessly to achieve it.

How many of these traits apply to you?
__ You follow through on personal and business commitments
__ You inspire others through your ideals

__ You take a quiet but persistent course of action
__ You lead through an organizational vision
__ You are known for your integrity and consistency of purpose
__ You approach both relationships and work idealistically
__ You prefer quiet and solitude for intense concentration
__ You work hard to make your inspirations a reality
__ You tend to win cooperation rather than demand it
__ You can organize complex interactions between people and tasks

Words to Live By: holistic, idealistic, loyal, intense, reserved, conceptual, committed, compassionate, deep, determined, sensitive, and creative.

Jobs and Careers That Attract Your Type: Human resources, business management, priest, career and educational counseling, psychologist, clergy, artist, writer, editor, teacher, designer, poet, social scientist, dietician, speech therapist, consulting, special education, librarian, welfare, benefits, abuse counseling, interpreter, diversity manager, marketer, and OD consulting,

Words You Use to Describe Yourself:_____

Extended Profile: Yours is one of the most thoughtful and thought full of the sixteen types. Few people are as happy, as you, in the world of pure ideas. When working on projects, your passion for perfection drives you and those working with you. Indeed, you may over work reworking all the details until everything is just right, and from your perspective, it rarely is. Sometimes this demand for unrealistic perfection can get in the way of your normal creativity, imagination, and invention.

Usually, you focus on possibilities and relate those possibilities to people. Where people and values are concerned, you are tenacious. You will go to great lengths to help, promote, facilitate, and assist others with less power or privilege.

In both your personal and business life, you live, eat, sleep, breathe, people and values. As a powerful people motivator, you understand human motivations and read others with exquisite clarity. Indeed, you often strike others as being downright psychic in knowing what others are thinking without their articulating it.

You probably see yourself as a seeker of truth. As such you are drawn to personal development and continual self-assessment. Finding a way to integrate yourself with the world around you gives you a sense of peace and well-being. There is often a strong spiritual side to your personality, as well; one, not so much rooted in religion, as in understanding the spiritual nature of the world and its possibilities.

As a leader, you seek to develop others who manage without pretense. Since you, yourself, place a high premium on being sincere, relating to others without masks is very important to you. Similarly, you encourage those who work for you to have the same degree of authenticity with their employees. That approach usually requires that your organization have a clear sense of purpose, clearly stated values, and a vision to guide you.

Relationships are your primary focus. You would love to have your affections reciprocated, but if they are not, you are willing to spend yourself regardless. Casual relationships are of little interest to you; instead, the deep, dedicated, and intense friendships you develop often amaze others. You are much less interested in having several friendships, than a few intense ones.

When others tell you that only animals have instincts, not humans, you are skeptical and perplexed. It has seemed natural to you to have certain instinctual reactions to circumstances and people. Some strike you as evil and others good with no apparent data to back you up. The eerie thing is that you are usually right.

The right workplace for you is quiet and harmonious. Tension and bureaucracy stifle you and crush your creativity. You will strive to promote harmony and act as a peacemaker when tensions arrive. When others are harmed, you will tend to take it personally and strike a sense of righteous indignation if the situation cannot be rectified. Reprimanding an employee is usually difficult for you, and while you are happy to praise others, bearing bad news is quite difficult.

At home, you will tend to idealize the situation. You may dote on your children and exude affection. You will want the home to be safe and without tension. You may tend to idealize your relationship and be crushed if children do not live up to your expectations and your mate is less than perfect.

Yours is a busy life, and you most likely will wind up over-committing yourself: human resources vice president by day and volunteer director of the crisis hotline in the evenings; elementary school teacher by day and volunteer at the women's shelter in the evenings; chemical engineer by day and an America's Promise volunteer mentor for center city youth three afternoons a week. And when the telephone rings for someone to collect for the Heart Fund, play the piano for the school holiday concert, or hand out t-shirts for the AID's March on Saturday, you are ready to volunteer.

Type and Age: Although you have elected just four preferences as your "type," life is an ongoing experience of learning how to use all eight preferences at the appropriate time, for the appropriate task. You will develop different preferences at specific, predictable times in your life.

For your type, the flow is as follows:

Dominant—introverted iNtuition (ages 8-15)

Auxiliary—extraverted Feeling (ages 16-30)

Tertiary—introverted Thinking (ages 31-40)

Inferior—extraverted Sensing (ages 41-55)

What we refer to as your Dominant function is iNtuition, which you express internally. To do your best work, you need quiet alone time to develop ideas and think about the future. You probably developed this function first from the ages 8-15. When you come to closure about the ideas that have enriched your world, you use your Auxiliary function, which is Feeling judgment. This function is expressed in the outer world; hence, you extravert it. This function was likely developed between the ages of 16-30. Hence, by the end of college or the beginning of your early professional years, the iNtuitive–Feeling ground floor to your personality has been laid. The middle two letters of your personality become the team of preferences that you will trust the most into the beginning of midlife.

About the age of 31, one of your non-preferences asks to be dealt with. We call it your Tertiary function. For your type, it is Thinking judgment, which you introvert. Your best decision making relative to analysis and logic, will be done alone, in the internal world. Others may not know you are reflecting on such concerns, but they will be very important to you. From the ages of 31-40, you develop this interest in analytical thinking. Your type does not change, but you learn how to use this non-preference when required. Your last preference to be developed we call the Inferior function. For you, it is Sensing, which you extravert. During the ages of 41-55, you will become more comfortable trading in data and facts in the public arena.

Type, then, is far more than just 4 letters on a report form. If all goes well, and it rarely does, by late midlife, you will have developed the capacity to use each of the 8 preferences when needed, with some degree of sophistication. We call this process the full development of type.

Type Under Stress: Under heavy stress, you tend to get bogged down with irrelevant details. Normally, when using your dominant introverted intuitive function, you look easily to the future, tackle new problems with excitement, and act ingeniously to solve problems. When you suddenly get trapped working out of your inferior function, which is extraverted Sensing, everything changes. You become preoccupied with data and facts that normally you would have dismissed. You may obsess about dieting, exercising, hedge pruning, eating, or drinking. Overindulging becomes the norm. A sense of drivenness pervades your work. Whatever you do is expressed feverishly. You clean the house till 2:00 am, rearrange the spice rack for hours, iron until your arm falls asleep, or become obsessed with balancing the checkbook. You may rant and rave and even verbally attack those closest to you. You may feel childish and accuse others of never helping you or loving you.

Your Type and Ethics: Values are very important to you. You see yourself as being incredibly value-centered.

Indeed people and values are your focus. Let's admit, however, that values for you can be a little bit "gray," in the best sense of the term. The term situation ethics best describes your normal approach to valuing. Despite the rule or the principle that may have been violated, you may want to decide differently for each person involved depending on who is at stake or what values have been assailed. The value is invested in the person, not the abstract rule. This approach to ethical behavior can sometimes get you in hot water for seeming too soft or too fickle, in the eyes of others, when all the issues are surfaced. If that happens, so be it; for you, the human being is the most important consideration. Given the choice between justice and mercy, mercy usually gets your nod.

Other INFJ's who you know:_____

INTJ
Conceptualizer, Improver, Scientist, Director
Global Strategic Innovator

Overview: You have indicated that you prefer Introversion, iNtuition, Thinking, and Judging as your favorite ways of dealing with the world around you. By selecting those preferences, you join about 1% of the world's population who share the same personality type.

Other High Performers who share your type include: Richard Nixon, General Alexander Haig, Vice President Dick Cheney, Condaleeza Rice, Roslyn Carter, Al Gore, Katharine Hepburn, Governor Michael Dukakis, Tommy Lee Jones, Thomas Edison, Henry Kissinger, Jack Welsh, and David Letterman.

Snapshot: You are perhaps the most fiercely independent and skeptical of the sixteen types and are single-minded and determined in pursuit of your vision despite any skepticism or opposition that you may face. Frank Sinatra's "My Way" is your theme song.

Leadership Style: Your type is one of the four most likely to rise to the top of large and complex organizations. In Fortune 500 Companies, your type comprises about 26 % of all CEO's, 9.8 % of all senior and executive vice presidents, and 7.2 % of middle managers. You are known for your personal drive and intellectual intensity in achieving it. Any time someone shows you a project or shares with you an idea, you can improve it. Even the very best in your world can be made better. Self-sufficiency and independence are your hallmarks, and you value that same trait in your subordinates whom you will constantly challenge to become better and more competent. You have

31

great drive towards personal and professional goals. In the organization, you believe strongly that one's authority derives from personal competence, not an assigned position.

How many of these traits apply to you?

__ You like to organize ideas into action

__ You are easily frustrated by others' plodding approach to problems

__ You have a strong, clear vision of the organization's future

__ You tend to drive yourself and others to achieve

__ You can be quite tough-minded with others

__ You prefer to conceptualize, design and build challenging models

__ Reorganizing the entire enterprise is a task you enjoy

__ You provide strong, clear conceptual design skills

__ You naturally think systemically and push others to attain the same mind set

__ You will work to remove any obstacle to achieve your personal and business goals

Words to Live By: creative, global, demanding, visionary, systems-minded, critical, independent, autonomous, private, theoretical, firm, original, and logical.

Jobs and Careers That Attract Your Type: Scientist, business leader, economist, inventor, designer, architect, writer, graphics designer, editor, engineering (chemical, civil, metallurgical), judge, consulting, strategic planner, attorney (intellectual property), university professor, mathematician, biomedical research, astronomer, computer systems expert, international banking, telecommunications, marketing, investment strategist, design engineer, operations research, concert pianist or violinist, new business developer, senior manager, curriculum designer, software and hardware systems designer, and orchestra director or conductor.

Words You Use to Describe Yourself:_____

Extended Profile: Yours is the most fiercely independent of all the sixteen types. You are conceptual, theoretical, intellectual, and self- confident. You live in the rich world of ideas and can stubbornly pursue your vision and dreams, even in the face of criticism and overwhelming pressure to conform. Such conformity to the status quo does not impress you.

Chances are that in your growing up years, you found yourself on the outside of most cliques and social groups. Your individualism and stubborn independence may have kept you out of many of the experiences shared by the more extraverted kids in your class.

Clearly, you believe in yourself and in your vision of the way things ought to be. If you have critics, you choose not to hear them because of the passionate belief you have in your own abilities. You are sometimes dumfounded by others' inability to see things as clearly as you.

Life is a lifetime of learning for you, and you believe it should be for others as well. Because of this belief, others may disappoint you on a regular basis because they are not as zealous to learn as you are. The idea of multiple intelligences and their constituents may fascinate you, and once you determine where your innate strengths lie, you may constantly chart and list things you want to learn, disciplines you want to conquer, and systems you desire to change. The world is your oyster, and you can find yourself successful in any number of different professions, although those of a technical nature probably appeal to you more than others.

As a leader, a parent, and a spouse you can often set extraordinarily high standards for yourself and others. It is very hard for others to live up to your expectations. Because you are a natural critic, when your teenager brings home a report card with five A's and a B, you know the first question you are going to ask. Likewise in the workplace, the INTJ is one of the types known for giving the lowest performance appraisals of all the types. That's because you are also giving the same report to yourself; you can always improve, and you run the risk of programming yourself for failure because you can't live up to your own standards.

You tend to be a very private individual and prefer a quiet working environment so you can lose yourself in thought while working. You really do not expect others to understand you; you believe that is their problem, after all, not yours. In your work life, you prefer a job that lets you shift your efforts from project to project, but curiously, at home, if you begin a project, you are often single-minded in your zeal to finish it without rest, without break, without stopping for a Diet Coke. You tell yourself that this kind of work at home is your therapy for unwinding, but you realize, when pushed, you never really relax. When you play, you work at playing.

Meetings are a real challenge for you because you despise repetition and valueless time. As you hear presentation after presentation, you have the ability to filter out the extraneous and zero in on the essentials, like an owl diving for the scurrying mouse. Twenty minutes into a two-hour meeting, you are sure what the conclusion should be and instead count the number of times a speaker says "uh," removes his glasses, scratches her chin, or makes grammatical mistakes. Once you determine a presenter is incompetent, you have no further need to pay attention to her. On the one hand, you are so intuitively astute, that your judgments about the outcome are probably warranted. On the other hand, you may run the risk of jumping to conclusions too quickly. That can hurt your judgment and the organization's success.

Type and Age: Although you have elected just four preferences as your "type," life is an ongoing experience of learning how to use all eight preferences at the appropriate time, for the appropriate task. You will develop different preferences at specific, predictable times in your life.

For your type, the flow is as follows:

Dominant—introverted iNtuition (ages 8-15)

Auxiliary—extraverted Thinking (ages 16-30)

Tertiary—introverted Feeling (ages 31-40)

Inferior—extraverted Sensing (ages 41-55)

What we refer to as your Dominant function is iNtuition, which you express internally. To do your best work, you need quiet, alone time to reflect on the models, theories, and possibilities available to help you. You probably developed this preference first, between the ages 8-15. When you judge and analyze the data, you use your Auxiliary function, which is Thinking judgment. This function is expressed in the outer world; hence, you extravert it. This function was likely developed between the ages of 16-30. Hence, by the end of college or beginning of your early professional years, the iNtuitive–Thinking ground floor to your personality has been laid. The middle two letters of your personality type become the team of preferences that you will trust the most into the beginning of midlife.

About the age of 31, one of your non-preferences asks to be dealt with. We call it your Tertiary function. For your type, it is Feeling judgment, which you introvert. Your best decision making, relative to personal, value-related concerns, will be done alone, in the internal world. Others may not know you are reflecting on such concerns, but they will be very important to you. From the ages of 31 to about 40 you will develop this capacity to empathize. You type does not change, but you learn how to use this non-preference when required. During the development of your Feeling function, it can be a fairly emotional time because your use of this function is not very sophisticated. Your last preference to be developed we call the Inferior function. For you, it is Sensing, which you extravert. During the ages of 41-55 you will become more comfortable trading in the external world of data, facts, and specifics, and those around you may become aware of your increased need to see such data before making decisions.

Type, then, is far more than just 4 letters on a report form. If all goes well, and it rarely does, by late midlife, you will have developed the capacity to use each of the 8 preferences when needed, with some degree of sophistication. We call this process the full development of type.

Type Under Stress: Under heavy stress, your type tends to get obsessed with irrelevant details. Normally when using your dominant introverted iNtuitive function, you are focused clearly on the future, you watch out for opportunities, and approach problem situations enthusiastically. When you suddenly get trapped working out of your inferior function, which is extraverted Sensing, everything changes. When speaking in stressful situation, you may tend to babble; your normally lucid prose sounds silly. Insignificant data bothers you, and you become obsessed at developing more. You will over exercise, over eat, and perhaps drink excessively. Sometimes you can actually do physical harm to yourself. You will yell instead of explain quietly and rationally. Ranting and raving, something you would never think about doing, normally, suddenly seems to make sense. Almost in a childish way, you blame others in absolute terms: "You always... You never..."

Your Type and Ethics: Your approach to deciding what ethical behavior encompasses often surprises others. Values are incredibly important to you, and you often make that fact clear to others who live and work with you; however, values mean something altogether different to you than to other types. The persons involved or the rules that are broken are mostly irrelevant to you. What is important is the principle at stake, beneath the rules. In fact, you may be willing to break any rule or law that exists, as long as there is a clearer principle at stake behind the rule. Indeed, you may see the rules as merely arbitrary impediments to ethical behavior. You are willing to challenge them just as you would challenge any other arbitrary system. Once the principle at stake is clear, so is your necessary action. With ethics, as with most things in this life, you will seem antiauthoritarian and self-willed. For you, that is just fine.

Other INTJ's who you know:_____

ISTP

Operator, Risk Taker, Artisan, Analyzer

Hands-On Practical Problem Solver

Overview: You have indicated that you prefer Introversion, Sensing, Thinking, and Perceiving as your favorite ways of dealing with the world around you. By selecting those preferences, you join about 6% of the world's population who share the same personality type.

Other High Performers who share your type include: Red Adair, General Stonewall Jackson, Evel Knievel, Sandra Bullock, Sam Donaldson, and Burt Reynolds.

Snapshot: You are practical and logical in approaching both work and relationships. Totally aware of the facts and rooted in the moment, you are adept at managing situations that require immediate attention.

Leadership Style: In Fortune 500 Companies, your type comprises 8.6 % of presidents and CEO's, 4.3 % of senior and executive vice presidents, and 4.1 % of middle managers. Actions are more important than words for you, and you lead by example. Picture the civil war company commander riding in front of the troops, sword in hand, leading them into battle. That is your favorite position. You lead by example and rise to the occasion to do whatever is necessary to ensure mission success. You remain calm during crises, and others look to you for your calming effect during stressful times. When you lead, you have no desire to micromanage and tend to manage loosely and by exception.

How many of these traits apply to you?

__ You remain calm during crises and become better as things get worse

__ You tend to get things done despite the rules, not because of them

__ You enjoy the trouble-shooting process and like to play detective in technical problems

__ You prefer a cooperative team atmosphere where everyone is a peer

__ You prefer to manage loosely because you, yourself, prefer minimal supervision

__ Data is your real strength, and others frequently check with you because they know you will have the facts at hand

__ Your calm behavior during crises has a settling effect on others

__ You have a natural proclivity for technical issues

__ You like to know your job, but do not want to be told how to do your job

__ You tend to manage by general operating principles rather than specific rules or procedures

Words to Live By: self-determined, spontaneous, independent, analytical, realistic, expedient, adaptable, adventurous, applied, factual, practical, and logical.

Jobs and Careers That Attract Your Type: Economist, accountant, legal secretary, computer repair, airline mechanic, coach, carpenter, office manager, banker, management consultant, electronics specialist, marine biologist, computer programming, purchasing agent, paralegal, farmer, commercial artist, radiology technician, dental assistant, fire fighter, police officer, race car driver, pilot, CIA field agent, surveyor, private investigator, engineering (electrical, mechanical, civil), and emergency medical technician.

Words You Use to Describe Yourself:_____

Extended Profile: Yours is one of the most practical of the sixteen types. You have the knack for responding to whatever comes down the pike with cool objectivity. You have little need to control events or people around you; you "just do it" and do it well. The right approach for you is the one that works. You tend to see yourself as an independent thinker and are little concerned about what others may think.

You have never been one to show your feelings, even to those for whom you care the most. In fact, it is probably hard for you to believe that others need as much affection as they do. You have always seen yourself as a kind of rugged individualist and therefore may forget to give others the pat on the back or the kind compliment for things you simply see as doing their duty. Others may see you being critical, therefore, for just not being effusive in your appreciation.

While you do not go out of the way to make friends, when you have one it is a friend for life. Feelings have little to do with it; you will "be there" for that friend, come Hell or high water. It is the kind of commitment that drives a pilot never to leave his wingman, a racecar driver to trust his pit crew with his life, or a trial attorney to trust her law clerk. All of these jobs, by the way, appeal to your type in large numbers.

When you work on a task, you do not mind being told what your job is; you just do not want to be told how to do that job. As long as the job is one of your choosing, you will look to others like you are driven, disciplined, and goal directed. You would never describe yourself that way to others; you just know that you are enjoying what you are doing, and therefore may stay immersed in the task until it is completed.

Commitment is a problematic area for you. When something appeals to you, you are more committed than most, but when your interest in a task wanes, your desire to finish it goes as well. Let's think about relationships. When you are interested or excited, you are "there" for all you are worth, but when the relationship goes stale, when the imposed "to do" list gets too long, when the obligations become overwhelming, your interest in staying slips quickly and you feel a strong desire to pick up stakes and move on.

Whereas boredom causes you to lose all interest, a nail-biting crisis brings out your best. Where the situation is at its worst and most confusing, you are at your clearest. Working moment by moment, figuring things out on the run, probably excites you. You simply thrive on action, regardless of whether that takes you to the emergency room, the skunk works, the battlefield, the negotiating table, the oil rig, the stage, or the annual investors' meeting.

Even if your job does not entail technology, you probably enjoy tinkering with "stuff." For fun, you tear down your '55 T-bird's engine over the weekend, build your own deck, redesign your low voltage garden lights, or play your daughter a video baseball game on MLB 2003. Games and adult toys probably have a real appeal to you, as does some weekend sport: golf, fishing, skeet-shooting, stock car racing, or ice sailing.

At work, you want a quiet place to work. If the telephone never rings, you are quite happy. Because of your introversion, you have no need to have others around you and may feel limited or stifled when they are. If you have to communicate with others, you prefer some kind of written communication—e-mail, memo, or note—to verbal confrontations. If possible, you prefer to let others—secretary, publicist, or aide—handle such communications for you.

You excel at precise work, and others trust you to be correct when you cite data or information. Others' ideas, visions, and theories, quite frankly, worry you. It is difficult to trust something you can't see or touch.

You do not need to be treated personally. You just want to be treated fairly. You will take it from there. Because of your keen analytical abilities, you have what it takes to go quite far in the military, business, and politics.

Type and Age: Although you have elected just four preferences as your "type," life is an ongoing experience of learning how to use all eight preferences at the appropriate time, for the appropriate task. You will develop different preferences at specific, predictable times in your life.

For your type, the flow is as follows:

Dominant—introverted Thinking (ages 8-15)

Auxiliary—extraverted Sensing (ages 16-30)

Tertiary—introverted iNtuition (ages 31-40)

Inferior—extraverted Feeling (ages 41-55)

What we refer to as your Dominant function, is Thinking judgment, which you express internally. To do your best work, you need quiet, alone time to analyze, ponder and come to closure. You probably developed this preference first, between the ages 8-15. When you actually look at the data and information required for you to do your best decision-making, you use your Auxiliary function, which is Sensing. This function is expressed in the outer world; hence, you extravert it. This function was likely developed between the ages of 16-30. Hence, by the end of college or beginning of your early professional years, the Thinking–Sensing ground floor to your personality has been laid. The middle two letters of your personality type become the team of preferences that you will trust the most into the beginning of midlife.

About the age of 31, one of your non-preferences asks to be dealt with. We call it your Tertiary function. For your type, it is iNtuition, which you introvert. Your best ideas, concepts, theories, and models will come to you while you are alone, in your internal world. Others may not know you are reflecting on such esoteric concerns, but they will be very important to you. From the ages of 31 to about 40 you will develop this capacity to dwell in the world of ideas. Your type does not change, but you learn how to use this non-preference when required. Your last preference to be developed we call the Inferior function. For you, it is Feeling judgment, which you extravert. During the ages of 41-55 you will become more comfortable trading in the interpersonal world of people and values.

Type, then, is far more than just 4 letters on a report form. If all goes well, and it rarely does, by late midlife, you will have developed the capacity to use each of the 8 preferences when needed, with some degree of sophistication. We call this process the full development of type.

Type Under Stress: Under heavy stress, you are likely to become overly sensitive and react negatively to any criticism. Normally, when using your dominant function, which is introverted Thinking, you are a keen and careful analyst. If you face opposition, you will react in a level-headed, rational way. You abide by the policies, and fix problems before they become major concerns. When you suddenly get trapped working out of your inferior function, which is extraverted Feeling, everything changes. You may forget things and become generally disorganized. You mislay your car keys, lose your purse, or forget your wallet. You become overly emotional. You will become angry over small things, yell, and over personalize any criticisms of your work or style. Touchy, touchy, touchy! That small problem you have to solve? You can't put it down; you can't stop working at it. And, while you can't stop working away at it, you feel totally disorganized in everything you do.

Your Type and Ethics: You are often surprised by others who get worked up over abstract ethical principles or the need to legislate our moral behavior with some code of behavior. For you, what works is right. You are one of the most pragmatic of the sixteen types, and that pragmatism prevails over arbitrary rules. To be quite frank, you tend to be suspicious of those who try to establish core values for a company or legislate behavior at any level of our society. When a situation arises in which you have to decide right or wrong, you trust yourself to know what to do. All the codification of rules accomplishes is the creation of a system of sanctions by which others can second-guess your behavior. That seems stupid to you. Principles, values, ethics, and morality are all slippery and esoteric concepts for you. You just want to be accepted for who you are and judged by what you do. "Just do it," is the most important value in the workplace.

Other ISTP's who you know:_____

ISFP
Composer, Psychic, Artist, Producer
Seer and Feeler of the Unseen

Overview: You have indicated that you prefer Introversion, Sensing, Feeling, and Perceiving as your favorite ways of dealing with the world around you. By selecting those preferences, you join about 6 % of the world's population who share the same personality type.

Other High Performers who share your type include: Ernest Hemingway, Charlie Brown, comedian George Carlin, Steven Segal, Saint Francis of Assisi, and Michael Jackson.

Snapshot: Kindness and compassion towards those less fortunate than yourself help you to extend yourself in a gentle way towards others. You are open-minded and deal with other people and events that come along in a flexible and caring way.

Leadership Style: In Fortune 500 Companies, your type comprises less than 1 % of presidents and CEO's, 1.1 % of senior and executive vice presidents, and 1.5 % of middle managers. You have very little need to control or lead others, and your style is to motivate others on the basis of personal loyalty. Your natural tendency is to trust others implicitly, and you will tend to redirect others' efforts by motivating them rather than criticizing their behavior. You value harmony and teamwork and have an egalitarian approach to others.

How many of these traits apply to you?
__ You act humanistically to ensure others' well being

__ Your style is to persuade others gently rather than to direct them

__ Whatever the situation, you rise to the occasion and do what is necessary

__ You are much more likely to praise than to criticize

__ You naturally generate personal loyalty in others

__ Team work and cooperation are your preferred work styles

__ As others' needs become apparent, you act to attend to them

__ You have almost a psychic understanding of human motivations

__ A workplace where you and others can work quietly and happily is your favorite atmosphere

__ You are a natural facilitator of others, and you bring people and tasks together with uncommon skill

Words to Live By: harmonious, spontaneous, loyal, observant, adaptable, gentle, understanding, trusting, cooperative, sensitive, modest, and caring.

Jobs and Careers That Attract Your Type: Bookkeeper, teacher, chef, crisis hotline operator, storekeeper, exercise physiologist, optometrist, optician, beautician, travel coordinator, interior designer, customer service specialist, LPN, marine biologist, forest ranger, veterinarian, emergency medicine specialist, paramedic, dancer, painter, artist, physical therapist, massage therapist, botanist, surveyor, home health care sales, cleaning service operator, fashion designer, gardener, potter, sports equipment sales, and alcohol and drug counselor.

Words You Use to Describe Yourself:_____

Extended Profile: The very traits that you pride yourself on so greatly may not always be apparent to those who work with you. Sensitivity, warmth, and personal commitment to others, that so inform your approach to work and relationships, often lie guarded beneath a tough veneer formed from your sensing and perceptive approach to life.

What often lies even deeper beneath those traits is a keen sense of personal morality. It is a morality not based so much on religion as on a keen personal sense of what is right or wrong. This moral view of the world causes you to take your duty seriously and treat your relationships lovingly.

Don't hear this morality as being anything mushy. Yours is one of the most practical of the sixteen types. Should anyone try to take advantage of your good will or violate one of your core principles, they will see immediately how practical you can become. Your normal openness and sensitivity can be replaced by rigidity and inflexibility. Values, after all, are to be taken seriously!

You are an intensely private person, and even those who are closest to you have a difficult time getting to know you. You tend to shelter your emotions, because they too, are meant to be personal and private. But when you are a friend, you are a friend to the bitter end. If, ten years from now, a person who you haven't seen for all those years needs help, you will be there.

In work, you thrive on jobs that allow you to have space and freedom. You like to have time to think, indeed contemplate sometimes, before you act, but when you act, it will be decisively. One of your questions is usually "when?" The answer is always, "now"! You are one of those types who is an immediate, practical, hands-on problem solver, trouble-shooter, and negotiator.

When others are faced with complex tasks, they may do substantial research, set long-term and short-term goals, assign roles and responsibilities, and practice their approach. All that strikes you as irrelevant and a waste of time. You know the best way to learn the complexity of the assignment is to jump in and start doing something and learn as you go. The important data will surface and the irrelevant will get disposed of in the process. You simply do what needs to be done.

Understanding this practical and hands-on approach to work, is the key to understanding your great strengths as a leader and professional. While you have a great capacity to "cut through the crap" you also have the empathy to understand others' motivations. You encourage others to attack tasks with zeal and energy. When they go astray or make mistakes, you are willing to redirect them rather than censure them. You work and care passionately and expect others to do the same. This sense of élan, some might call it esprit de corps, pervades your work style and team approach. It is all for one and one for all. To others in your group, union, team, fraternal organization, shift, or company, you will be unconditionally loyal.

All that is not to say that you are not frustrated sometimes by others' plodding approach to work, sterile approach to relationships, and bureaucratic stuffiness. Indeed, when the bureaucracy burgeons and the silly commitments become too great, they have just lost you. Sometimes they just lose your vitality; other times, you will pick up stakes and move on. The Australian idea of simply "going walk-about," on the spur of the moment, has a real appeal to you.

Usually, your type has a real affinity for the natural world.

Because of your stated preferences, you tend to understand the signals your body is sending you far better than most and know you are ill long before your friendly Georgetown physician or his plethora of tests. You can probably isolate exactly where that bug is. At the same time, your type often has a real sense of what animals are going through. I'd much rather trust my pet to an ISFP high school graduate interning in the back of the veterinary clinic, than to a full-fledged vet with a couple of graduate degrees. For the same reason, your type often goes to or works with practitioners of all kinds of alternative medicine from chiropractory to kinesiology to acupuncture.

Hiking the Appalachian Trail, snowboarding the back bowls of Park City, Utah, or climbing one of the 15,000 foot mountains in Colorado is right down your alley. You do it not so much for the challenge, which can be part of your type, but for the peace and quiet and the chance to commune with God's grandeur.

What is certain is that you will always be open to novelty, able to adjust to changing work circumstances, and careful to include others in your decision making. There is probably not a prejudiced bone in your body, and you learned a long time ago the value of diversity in the work place. After all, it started with your need to be accepted as the very different person you are.

Type and Age: Although you have elected just four preferences as your "type," life is an ongoing experience of learning how to use all eight preferences at the appropriate time, for the appropriate task. You will develop different preferences at specific, predictable times in your life.

For your type, the flow is as follows:

Dominant—introverted Feeling (ages 8-15)
Auxiliary—extraverted Sensing (ages 16-30)
Tertiary—introverted iNtuition (ages 31-40)
Inferior—extraverted Thinking (ages 41-55)

What we refer to as your Dominant function is Feeling judgment, which you express internally. To do your best work, you need quiet, alone time to value and consider whom or what values might be at stake in your decision making. You probably developed this preference first, between the ages 8-15. When you gather the data necessary to warrant those personal and interpersonal decisions, you use your Auxiliary function, which is Sensing. This function is expressed in the outer world; hence, you extravert it. This function was likely developed between the ages of 16-30. Thus, by the end of college or beginning of your early professional years, the Feeling–Sensing ground floor to your personality has been laid. The middle two letters of your personality type become the team of preferences that you will trust the most into the beginning of midlife.

About the age of 31, one of your non-preferences asks to be dealt with. We call it your Tertiary function. For your type, it is iNtuition, which you introvert. As you consider other possibilities or models which may be appropriate in making sense of the data, you prefer to do this alone, in the internal world. Others may not know you are reflecting on such concerns, but they will be very important to you. From the ages of 31 to about 40 you will develop this capacity to explore your world of ideas. Your type does not change, but you learn how to use this non-preference when required. Your last preference to be developed we call the Inferior function. For you, it is Thinking judgment, which you extravert. During the ages of 41-55 you will become more comfortable performing the cooler, more hard-headed analysis that often must accompany our decision making.

Type, then, is far more than just 4 letters on a report form. If all goes well, and it rarely does, by late midlife, you will have developed the capacity to use each of the 8 preferences when needed, with some degree of sophistication. We call this process the full development of type.

Type Under Stress: Under heavy stress, you may become unusually domineering and obstinate. Normally, when using your dominant function, which is introverted Feeling, you are one of the most empathic of the sixteen types. You are capable of anticipating how others will feel and react and are careful to take that knowledge into consideration. You appreciate others' contributions and keep values always in your headlights. When you suddenly get trapped working out of your inferior function, which is extraverted Thinking judgment, everything changes. You become critical and carping of others. You may lose objectivity and find fault with virtually everything. If you are in charge, you will stop listening to others and act arbitrarily. That unconscious fear you have always had of personal failure now starts getting projected on to others. Everything seems impossible, and you begin to lose faith in your ability to perform even the simplest task.

Your Type and Ethics: You are often surprised by others who get worked up over abstract ethical principles or the need to legislate our moral behavior with some code of behavior. For you, what works is right. You are one of the most pragmatic of the sixteen types, and that pragmatism prevails over arbitrary rules. To be quite frank, you tend to be suspicious of those who try to establish core values for a company or legislate behavior at any level of our society. When a situation arises in which you have to decide right or wrong, you trust yourself to know what to do. All the codification of rules accomplishes is the creation of a system of sanctions by which others can second-guess your behavior. That seems stupid to you. Principles, values, ethics, and morality are all slippery and esoteric concepts for you. You just want to be accepted for who you are and judged by what you do. "Just do it," is the most important value in the workplace.

Other ISFP's who you know:_____

INFP
Harmonizer, Servant, Quester, Clarifier
Empathic, Value-Centered Helper

Overview: You have indicated that you prefer Introversion, iNtuition, Feeling, and Perceiving as your favorite ways of dealing with the world around you. By selecting those preferences, you join about 1% of the world's population who share the same personality type.

Other High Performers who share your type include: Isabel Briggs Myers, Mahatma Gandhi, Abraham Lincoln, Joan of Arc, and psychologist Carl Rogers.

Snapshot: You have an uncanny knack for knowing what others have not told you. You have a talent for listening but prefer to cast what you hear in the form of stories and metaphors laced with moral overtones. You will normally go with the flow until your core values come under attack; then you will act relentlessly to right the situation. Existence is a mystery for you, and you enjoy unraveling its many nuances. Life is a lifetime of coming to know yourself.

Leadership Style: In Fortune 500 Companies, your type comprises about 2.8 % of presidents and CEO's, 1.5 % of senior and executive vice presidents, and 2.1 % of middle managers. You are perhaps the most idealistic of the sixteen types, and others frequently have a difficult time living up to your moral view of the universe. You have a rich sense of creativity and impress others by your almost profound sense of personal honor and concern for organizational values. In working with others, you prefer a facilitative approach and would like to motivate them by loyalty and values rather than impressing them with the rules.

Your leadership style is often unconventional, and you prefer to take a subtle, influential approach to motivating others.

How many of these traits apply to you?
__ You push quietly for clear organizational values
__ Praise of others comes easier for you than criticism
__ You prefer a facilitative role to a supervisory one
__ Finding the unique role for each individual is an important consideration for you
__ You can be quite persuasive with others about your values
__ Having a common purpose for a team or business motivates you
__ New ideas and possibilities help focus your energies
__ You, yourself, prefer a unique role rather than conventional ones
__ You tend to bring people together around you rather than around an abstract principle
__ You prefer an open, but solitary and quiet work place

Words to Live By: empathic, devoted, creative, virtuous, committed, gentle, compassionate, reticent, idealistic, loyal, adaptable, and kind.

Jobs and Careers That Attract Your Type: Psychology, consulting, conflict manager, senior business manager, speech therapist, librarian, human resources, diversity manager, clergy, counseling, psychiatry, missionary, holistic medicine, dietician, legal and couples mediation, nutritional counselor, nurse, social worker, researcher, college professor of humanities, bilingual specialist, preschool teaching, actor, artist, musician, religious educator, occupational therapist, massage therapist, employment development specialist, and nun.

Words You Use to Describe Yourself:_____

Extended Profile: You are, perhaps, the most idealistic of the sixteen types. You tend to expect that good, sound relationships will be without conflict, marriages will be based on deep mutual devotion, and employees will trust the leadership to act in value-centered, visionary ways. This view of the world encourages you to lead based on vision and values, but leaves you vulnerable to disappointment from those even close to you.

You tend to be a mostly private person, and others must work hard to earn the privilege of entering your inner world. Once you grant them that privilege, they will find a faithful and committed partner who acts on the foundation of a clear moral basis where the protagonists wear white and black hats. Values are usually that clear for you. A potential sore point for you is that such clarity of moral roles is seldom found in other types with whom you must interact.

Your circle of friends is smaller than for most. Many of those persons that your more extraverted associates would consider friends, are merely passing acquaintances for you. Once you let one in behind your veneer, you will hold their friendship dearly and be there as an unconditional buddy next year or fifteen years later. Time and distance will be no impediment for your commitment to them. Where you can be disappointed is in expecting others to be just as committed to you.

You have probably expended a great deal of energy over the years finding just the right job, just the right company, and just the right partner to be worthy of you and your passion. That job usually has a mission attached to it: save the soul, turn the failing business around, help the patient recover, or help the executive you are coaching become truly high performing.

Because you tend to be a very private person, others will often see your second best function when they deal with you. That function is intuition that allows you to be a great source of stimulating ideas, encouragement, and inspiration for others. Sadly, what others miss in focusing on this part of your personality that you choose to share, is your more important, but heavily guarded warmth and verve. They run the risk of seeing you as cooler and less passionate than you actually are.

Others are frequently surprised to know how perceptive you are in assessing motives in others. Being genuine matters greatly to you, so when you intuit a lack of candor in others, they tend to be "dead meat." You will not want to work with them again. Because you are one of the four types we refer to as empathists, you are superb at reading others' body language. You will hear the words coming out of someone's mouth and just know they are disingenuous at best or lying through their teeth at worst.

This desire to be a seeker of truth extends from your personal convictions to your work life. You will naturally look for hidden signals in those at the negotiating table, covert behaviors in business meetings, or personal agendas as people come together as a team. There is, in that regard, an almost psychic part to your personality. If someone of your type tells me that, although you have no evidence to support you, "you just know" that over in the shipping center in Dallas, TX, there are two people who are constantly at odds, and their relationship is destroying the morale of the entire business unit, I'll be booking an American Airlines flight tomorrow to check it out.

When you work, it is important to you to have a harmonious working environment. Contention and heavy-handed bureaucracy will shut you down. Because tension or argument in the workplace is destructive to you, you may tend to ignore it or, at worst, sweep it under the rug and hope it will go away. Just a tip; it won't!

Creativity is your long suit, and you will strive to find ways for the organization to benefit from your insights. While you have probably never found the perfect job, that fact does not discourage you from believing that such a one does exist, somewhere. This same tension exists between a world you know is based on a clear cut dichotomy between good and evil and the compromises you must make every day to work with very different people in the real world.

Because of your combination of preferences, you will want to consider all the angles, hear from all the parties involved, consider numerous courses of action, understand all the motivations and then act in a way consistent with your core values.

Type and Age: Although you have elected just four preferences as your "type," life is an ongoing experience of learning how to use all eight preferences at the appropriate time, for the appropriate task. You will develop different preferences at specific, predictable times in your life.

For your type, the flow is as follows:
Dominant—introverted Feeling (ages 8-15)
Auxiliary—extraverted iNtuition (ages 16-30)
Tertiary—introverted Sensing (ages 31-40)
Inferior—extraverted Thinking (ages 41-55)

What we refer to as your Dominant function, is Feeling judgment, which you express internally. To do your best work, you need quiet, alone time to decide and understand all the values and motivations that impact your decision. You may arrive at a value-centered decision before anyone else is aware of your decision. You probably developed this preference first, between the ages 8-15. When you reflect on all the ideas, models, and possibilities that help you see the world, you use your Auxiliary function, which is iNtuition. This function is expressed in the outer world; hence, you extravert it. This function was likely developed between the ages of 16-30. Hence, by the end of college or beginning of your early professional years, the Feeling–iNtuitive ground floor to your personality has been laid. The middle two letters of your personality type become the team of preferences that you will trust the most into the beginning of midlife.

About the age of 31, one of your non-preferences asks to be dealt with. We call it your Tertiary function. For your type, it is Sensing, which you introvert. Your best time gathering data, researching the pertinent information, or re-assaying the samples, will be done alone, in the internal world. Others may not know you are reflecting on such concerns, but they will be very important to you. From the ages of 31 to about 40 you will develop this capacity to deal with the sensate world. Your type does not change, but you learn how to use this non-preference when required. Your last preference to be developed we call the Inferior function. For you, it is Thinking judgment, which you extravert. During the ages of 41-55 you will become more comfortable trading in the external world of analysis, logical processes, and cause and effect decision-making.

Type, then, is far more than just 4 letters on a report form. If all goes well, and it rarely does, by late midlife, you will have developed the capacity to use each of the 8 preferences when needed, with some degree of sophistication. We call this process the full development of type.

Type Under Stress: Under heavy stress, you may become domineering, argumentative, and down right nasty. Normally, when using your dominant function, which is introverted Feeling judgment, you are kind, empathic, and appreciative. When you suddenly get trapped working out of your inferior function, which is extraverted Thinking, everything changes. Empathy gives way to anger and criticism. You take charge in an overbearing way and stop listening to what anyone says. You close yourself off to reality and create the reality you want. You will find fault with almost everything and react hypercritically. When others try to reason with you, you will become angry and accusatorial. You may become compulsive and try to organize everything and everyone according to your worldview. At worst, you are the only one who has the truth, and everyone else is wrong.

Your Type and Ethics: Values are very important to you. You see yourself as being incredibly value-centered. Indeed people and values are your focus. Let's admit, however, that values for you can be a little bit "gray," in the best sense of the term. The term situation ethics best describes your normal approach to valuing. Despite the rule or the principle that may have been violated, you may want to decide differently for each person involved depending on who is at stake or what values have been assailed. The value is invested in the person, not the abstract rule. This approach to ethical behavior can sometimes get you in hot water for seeming too soft or too fickle, in the eyes of others, when all the issues are surfaced. If that happens, so be it; for you, the human being is the most important consideration. Given the choice between justice and mercy, mercy usually gets your nod.

Other INFP's who you know:_____

INTP

Designer, Problem solver, Architect, Theorizer

Ignoring the Artificial Boundaries of Thought

Overview: You have indicated that you prefer Introversion, iNtuition, Thinking, and Perceiving as your favorite ways of dealing with the world around you. By selecting those preferences, you join about 1% of the world's population who share the same personality type.

Other High Performers who share your type include: Albert Einstein, David Keirsey, Carl Jung, Immanuel Kant, Woodrow Wilson, Linus (Peanuts character), and Theodore Waitt (Chairman of Gateway).

Snapshot: As one of the most theoretical of the sixteen types, you prefer to focus your energies on the abstract concept and the idea rather than on people or the immediate situation. You are curious, rational, and original in your thinking.

Leadership Style: In Fortune 500 Companies, your type comprises about 11.4 % of presidents and CEO's, 5.6 % of senior and executive vice presidents, and 4.9 % of middle managers. An unstructured approach to work and problem solving best suits your style. While emotions do not excite you, the intellect is a real turn on. As you lead and motivate others, you will do so on the basis of ideas, models, and concepts. The power of a new idea or framework for seeing reality excites you, and you trust it will excite others as well. Privacy, self- determination, and independence characterize your favorite work environment, and you tend to give others the same freedom of thought and action when you lead them.

How many of these traits apply to you?

___ You cut directly to the issue and let the chips fall where they may

___ Operating at the intellectual level rather than the emotional one turns you on

___ You like to apply logic and level-headed analysis to problem solving

___ You enjoy designing logical and complex organizations and systems

___ Your intellectual insights often amaze others

___ You prefer to lead independent thinkers and get frustrated by plodders

___ Expertise impresses you, not position or rank

___ You enjoy tackling complex problems

___ You are known for looking at new ways to impact traditional thinking

___ Organizing ideas excites you more than motivating people

Words to Live By: self-determined, original, independent, reserved, detached, skeptical, logical, cognitive, theoretical, speculative, and autonomous.

Jobs and Careers That Attract Your Type: Attorney, philosopher, logician, interpreter, economist, creative writing, artist, inventor, graphics designer, photographer, plastic surgery, management consulting, biomedical researcher, psychiatry, scientist, web designer, computer software designer, helicopter pilot, research and development, architect, legal mediator, financial analyst, new business development, university professor, network integration, financial planning, university faculty administrator, entertainer, and dancer.

Words You Use to Describe Yourself:_____

Extended Profile: More than once, you have probably been compared to the absent-minded professor. Your preference for solitary, alone work coupled with your delight in playing in the theoretical world of ideas, concepts, and possibilities allows you to lose yourself in an abstract and often intellectually rich world that few others can penetrate. You are at your best probing the complexities of the theoretical world, and when others try to tug you gently back to the tangibles of the real world, you can view them as intruding on your private world. Your response to others for entering your inner sanctum can sometimes be less than pleasant. You do not mean to be rude to others; you just do not engage them in the trite little pleasantries that others seem to like.

Once you have decided on a course of action or a theory to pursue, obstacles are no impediment. You side step them, ignore them, or treat them like a pesky fly to be brushed off as you pursue your vision. This ability to be single-minded in your efforts can win you kudos from others senior to you but can dismay colleagues and disappoint those reporting to you, because you will tend to leave them in your wake. Because you do not expect a lot of personal attention yourself, you tend, naturally, not to offer it to others as well. It is not that you do not care; it is just not a consideration that occurs to you.

Socially, as well as dealing with supervisors, you may have been told in the past that you lack tact. You are a speaker of truth. Small talk has never appealed to you; you go to the heart of the matter and point out the cockroach on the kitchen floor, the shaving cream in the ear, or the parent who blew the marriage. If there is a big, ugly, blue elephant in the corner of the room, you are not going to ignore it.

Your strategic business unit may have paid Boston

Consulting Company $ 300,000.00 for the strategic business plan they just delivered, but if the marketing piece doesn't make sense, you are going to question it, even though it is the president's sacred cow.

Although your type thrives in the world of computer science, research and development, and marketing, you are often most at home in the very thin air of university life— the more prestigious the university, the better. Yours is one of two types most likely to comprise the faculties of the better university graduate schools. When you speak to the "common folk," you can unconsciously project an air of intellectual arrogance. You may find yourself having to change your words and sentence structure to speak effectively with those who report to you. You will see this change as having to "dumb down" to accommodate others. If you do not, you may be seen as stuffy and unrealistic. Others just can't keep up with your grand sweep of universal concerns.

You are not one to decide too rapidly. Your perceptive nature coupled with your intuition makes you curious and open to many possibilities. You will encourage those who work for you to spread a wide net as they consider models that might be appropriate. If others cannot think creatively, you will challenge yourself and your own pet ideas, just to ensure that the truth emerges. You do not think outside the box; you generally dismantle it.

What is one of your great strengths is also your potential undoing. You often act on the basis of pure hunch—"theoretically...." Sometimes, you are wrong. You need to spend some time getting comfortable with justifying your decisions empirically.

Type and Age: Although you have elected just four preferences as your "type," life is an ongoing experience of learning how to use all eight preferences at the appropriate time, for the appropriate task. You will develop different preferences at specific, predictable times in your life.

For your type, the flow is as follows:
    Dominant—introverted Thinking (ages 8-15)
    Auxiliary—extraverted iNtuition (ages 16-30)
    Tertiary—introverted Sensing (ages 31-40)
    Inferior—extraverted Feeling (ages 41-55)

What we refer to as your Dominant function, is Thinking judgment, which you express internally. To do your best work, you need quiet, alone time to analyze, plan, and think logically about the consequences of your judgments. You probably developed this preference first, between the ages 8-15. You base your judgments on your stock of models, theories, and possibilities that are so important to you. When doing this, you use your Auxiliary function, which is iNtuition. This function is expressed in the outer world; hence, you extravert it. This function was likely developed between the ages of 16-30. Hence, by the end of college or beginning of your early professional years, the Thinking–iNtuitive ground floor to your personality has been laid. The middle two letters of your personality type become the team of preferences that you will trust the most into the beginning of midlife.

About the age of 31, one of your non-preferences asks to be dealt with. We call it your Tertiary function. For your type, it is your Sensing function, which you introvert. When you look at data, consider the facts bearing on the issues, or gather information, you prefer to do it alone, in the internal world. Others may not know you are reflecting on such concerns, but they will be very important to you. From the ages of 31 to about 40 you will develop this capacity to deal with the necessary data. Your type does not change, but you learn how to use this non-preference when required. Your last preference to be developed we call the Inferior function. For you, it is Feeling judgment, which you extravert. During the ages of 41-55 you will become more comfortable considering the more value-centered, interpersonal aspects of your decisions.

Type, then, is far more than just 4 letters on a report form. If all goes well, and it rarely does, by late midlife, you will have developed the capacity to use each of the 8 preferences when needed, with some degree of sophistication. We call this process the full development of type.

Type Under Stress: Under heavy stress, you tend to become angry and overly emotional. Normally, when using your dominant function, which is introverted Thinking, you are the consummate analyst. Personal attacks do not bother you, and you stand firm in the face of opposition. When you suddenly get trapped working out of your inferior function, which is extraverted Feeling, everything changes. You can become overly critical and feel under attack from all sides. You become very aware of your feelings and may become moody and impatient. You may yell or have other emotional outbursts and take any criticism personally. Many new emotions invade your world. You can feel maudlin and sentimental for no reason. Holidays may invoke a sense of sentimentality you never experienced before. You might even cry at a movie, God forbid. Often you do not even understand the source of your stress until sometime later, when things have subsided and returned to more-or-less normal.

Your Type and Ethics: Your approach to deciding what ethical behavior encompasses often surprises others. Values are incredibly important to you, and you often make that fact clear to others who live and work with you; however, values mean something altogether different to you than to other types. The persons involved or the rules that are broken are mostly irrelevant to you. What is important is the principle at stake, beneath the rules. In fact, you may be willing to break any rule or law that exists, as long as there is a clearer principle at stake behind the rule. Indeed, you may see the rules as merely arbitrary impediments to ethical behavior. You are willing to challenge them just as you would challenge any other arbitrary system. Once the principle at stake is clear, so is your necessary action. With ethics, as with most things in this life, you will seem antiauthoritarian and self-willed. For you, that is just fine.

Other INTP's Who You Know_____

ESTP
Expeditor, Realist, Promoter, Troubleshooter
Getting Better as Things Get Worse

Overview: You have indicated that you prefer Extraversion, Sensing, Thinking, and Perceiving as your favorite ways of dealing with the world around you. By selecting those preferences, you join about 13% of the world's population who share the same personality type.

Other High Performers who share your type include: General George Patton, Mit Romney (Chairman of the Salt Lake City Winter Olympics), Teddy Roosevelt, Lee Iacocca, Brett Favre (# 4, Green Bay Packers), Peppermint Patty (Peanuts Cartoon strip), and Governor Jesse Ventura.

Snapshot: You are resourceful, pragmatic, and realistic. Of all the sixteen types, you are perhaps the most action-oriented, hands-on practical problem solver of the lot. Working smarter not harder summarizes your approach to life.

Leadership Style: In Fortune 500 Companies, your type comprises about 2.8 % of presidents and CEO's, 3.4 % of senior and executive vice presidents, and 3.9 % of middle managers. Yours is one of the most entrepreneurial of the sixteen types, and you enjoy bringing together people, finances, and technology for new projects. You tend to be an outstanding negotiator and are often called upon to facilitate complicated business and financial deals. Intelligent compromise is your forte. A blunt, action-oriented person, you simply make things happen.

How many of these traits apply to you?

___ Risk taking is fun and comes easily to you

___ As situations become more dire, you excel

___ You are a natural negotiator, and you keep events in flux until they work out for your benefit

___ You understand the rules very clearly, but you also know when you have to break the rules to succeed

___ Your style is direct and assertive—no fluff here!

___ Your approach to problems is realistic and pragmatic

___ Short term goals are all you need to succeed; the long term ones are probably meaningless, anyhow

___ You like action and immediate results

___ Remembering and acting on the facts come easily to you

___ You become frustrated by those who just plod along. Your style is to make things happen!

Words to Live By: quick, pragmatic, persuasive, alert, versatile, adaptable, outgoing, easygoing, spontaneous, energetic, fun-loving, and activity-oriented.

Jobs and Careers That Attract Your Type: Pilot, entrepreneur, sportscasters, auditor, financial planner, budget analyst, labor negotiator, technology trainer, mechanic, marine biologist, network integration specialist, surveyor, radiological technician, corrections officer, insurance investigator, paramedic, fire fighter, land developer, general contractor, retail sales, management consulting, franchise owner, surveyor, chef, stockbroker, banker, reporter, auctioneer, professional athlete, private investigator, police officer, coach, real estate agent, exercise physiologist, corrections officer, emergency medical specialist, fireman, helicopter pilot, military special operations, race car driver, explosives expert, flight attendant, detective, bartender, fitness instructor, professional dancer, or musician.

Words You Use to Describe Yourself:_____

Extended Profile: Hands-on practical problem solver, troubleshooter, and negotiator. If these words begin to describe you, you have found the right profile. Of all the sixteen types, yours is the most rooted in reality, as you get the job done, regardless of the bureaucracy you have to slice through or the obstacles in your way. "Just do it," has always been your mantra.

As early as grade school and high school, you knew you were different. You learned differently. Other kids would be content to sit at their desks and work mimeograph after mimeograph. For you that was a huge waste of time. Most of the techniques the teachers prized so highly, you found boring. Attending lectures, practicing dozens of problems, reading three chapters in the science textbook, or memorizing a list of British kings and queens may have helped somebody learn, but they sure weren't for you. You didn't want to read about the water cycle, you wanted to make one. Studying pictures of a carburetor got you nowhere, but after you tore one apart in the automobile shop, you understood immediately how gas engines worked. Theories and essay exams were always less relevant than laboratory work where you could build, turn, tweak, titrate, or blow something up. You reversed the learning pattern and learned by doing. No one ever seemed to get that right. If you were told how something worked, that knowledge might last you for the third period, but if you could figure out how something worked, you would know it forever.

Just as you were practical in your approach to learning, so you are a good-natured realist on the job. Co-workers trust you to be grounded and not susceptible to the latest fad to come down the pike from headquarters. When others get worked up over the latest cause, the most recent catastrophe, some popular cult, or the latest foreign crisis, you stay the course with an equanimity that amazes all but your closest friends. They know that as things get worse, you get better. In a crisis, while others are panicking and running around frantically, you are at your best. You get easily bored by the status quo and routine, but you thrive on action.

You tend to be an enjoyer of life. Next year and next financial quarter will take care of themselves. You live for the moment, totally committed to your work and relationships, today. Tomorrow may be a different story. Some types like to separate the process from the product. For you, the two are one and the same.

When the restrictions of the job, the bureaucracy of the organization, or the commitments of the relationship become too burdensome, you start acting out of duty alone. This has never been your long suit, and you begin to feel restless. All it takes is one more meaningless requirement from headquarters, and you may be gone!

Working hard to save for that new bass boat, looking forward to the company party next June, or saving up for a new titanium golf club may strike some as fun, but you want it now. You probably invented the bumper sticker, "whoever dies with the most toys wins." It is not that you are greedy or avaricious—far from it. You are practical and live for the here and now. Others may work so they can have fun later. If you can't have fun while you are working, you will find something better to do.

Because you play as hard as you work, it is not at all unusual for some supervisor to walk through the manufacturing area and see you sitting down with your feet up on the desk. I advise them that unless this is routine behavior on your part, it is unwise for them to get upset about your down time. You tend to work in bursts of energy, and you relax the same way. You have probably done three times as much as anyone else before they arrive on the scene; they have just caught you relaxing just as hard.

Usually your type has a passion for jobs and careers that are traditionally thought of as being male occupations in our culture. Whether male or female, you are probably attracted to machines of all kinds: automobiles, helicopters, gadgets, adult toys, motorcycles, airplanes, and the like hold a fascination for many with your same preferences. If it is not in your work that you find yourself in a nontraditional role, it may be in relationships or in your leisure activities where you like to play sports, fish, race cars, drive boats, or rock climb on weekends. Your friends probably regard you as a very active person, even if it is just going to a baseball game instead of watching it on TV, or hiking the Appalachian Trail instead of reading National Geographic Magazine. If you are a woman, others probably saw you as a Tom boy as you grew up.

Everything you do, you tend to do harder and faster than your co-workers. The double whammy is that you prefer to work with others and have others around you in a team or work group, but you often get frustrated by having to slow down to accommodate them. You pay attention to the data and rarely make factual errors at work. But if the task requires the same routine to be done again and again, you get bored and may find yourself causing mistakes. Because, while you are great at solving problems—that is your forte—when there is no problem to solve, you are not above causing one, just to have something to do. Nowhere is that more true than at home where you can easily get bored by routine once it sets in.

Type and Age: Although you have elected just four preferences as your "type," life is an ongoing experience of learning how to use all eight preferences at the appropriate time, for the appropriate task. You will develop different preferences at specific, predictable times in your life.

For your type, the flow is as follows:

Dominant—extraverted Sensing (ages 8-15)

Auxiliary—introverted Thinking (ages 16-30)

Tertiary—extraverted Feeling (ages 31-40)

Inferior—introverted iNtuition (ages 41-55)

What we refer to as your Dominant function is Sensing, which you express externally. To do your best work, you spend time gathering data in meetings and among others in groups that you trust. Others you work with will hear you making requests for clear information. Your preference is to sort out all of this publicly, with the help of others. You probably developed this preference first, between the ages 8-15. When you judge and analyze the data, you use your Auxiliary function, which is Thinking. This function is expressed in the internal world; hence, you introvert it. You prefer quiet, alone time to perform your best, logical analysis. This function was likely developed between the ages of 16-30. Hence, by the end of college or beginning of your early professional years, the Sensing–Thinking ground floor to your personality has been laid. The middle two letters of your personality type become the team of preferences that you will trust the most into the beginning of midlife.

About the age of 31, one of your non-preferences asks to be dealt with. We call it your Tertiary function. For your type, it is Feeling judgments, which you extravert. Your best decision making, relative to personal, value-related concerns, will be done publicly, in the external world. Others may even be surprised that you are reflecting on such concerns, but they will begin to be important to you during this period. From the ages of 31 to about 40 you will develop the capacity to empathize. Your type does not change, but you learn how to use this non-preference when required. Your last preference to be developed we call the Inferior function. For you, it is iNtuition, which you introvert. During the ages of 41-55 you will become more comfortable thinking about ideas, visions, and possibilities, things which heretofore may have seemed extraneous, if not irrelevant, to you. When you use this function, you will do it in the internal world; hence, you introvert it.

Type, then, is far more than just 4 letters on a report form. If all goes well, and it rarely does, by late midlife, you will have developed the capacity to use each of the 8 preferences when needed, with some degree of sophistication. We call this process the full development of type.

Type Under Stress: Under heavy stress, you can easily get stuck in a rut and not see the forest for the trees. Normally, when using your dominant function, which is extraverted Sensing, you see immediately what needs attention and get it done. People expect you to be realistic when addressing problems. When you suddenly get trapped working out of your inferior function, which is introverted iNtuition, everything changes. You become unduly pessimistic and seem stuck with too many possibilities to unwind. Nothing gets done and you seem incapable of making up your mind. The future looks bleak, and you see the whole world in negative terms. You begin to have forebodings that your stock will crash, your loved one has cancer, or your child will be abducted. Fantasies of impending disasters fill your thoughts, and you begin to have self-doubts about completing the simplest of tasks.

Your Type and Ethics: You are often surprised by others

77

who get worked up over abstract ethical principles or the need to legislate our moral behavior with some code of behavior. For you, what works is right. You are one of the most pragmatic of the sixteen types, and that pragmatism prevails over arbitrary rules. To be quite frank, you tend to be suspicious of those who try to establish core values for a company or legislate behavior at any level of our society. When a situation arises in which you have to decide right or wrong, you trust yourself to know what to do. All the codification of rules accomplishes is the creation of a system of sanctions by which others can second-guess your behavior. That seems stupid to you. Principles, values, ethics, and morality are all slippery and esoteric concepts for you. You just want to be accepted for who you are and judged by what you do. "Just do it," is the most important value in the workplace.

Other ESTP's That You Know_____

ESFP
Motivator, Performer, Entertainer, Presenter
Optimistic, Fun, and Generous with Time and Talents

Overview: You have indicated that you prefer Extraversion, Sensing, Feeling, and Perceiving as your favorite ways of dealing with the world around you. By selecting those preferences, you join about 13% of the world's population who share the same personality type.

Other High Performers who share your type include: Richard Branson (Virgin Airlines), Steve Irwin (The Crocodile Hunter), Dagwood Bumstead (Blondie cartoon series), Geraldo Rivera, Gauguin (artist of Tahiti fame), and Suzanne Somers.

Snapshot: Fun loving, gregarious, and friendly, you are naturally drawn to people, and enjoy working with them on teams of all varieties. Long-term considerations take a back seat to acting immediately for the benefit of your organization and family.

Leadership Style: In Fortune 500 Companies, your type comprises about 2.8 % of presidents and CEO's, .8 % of senior and executive vice presidents, and 1.1 % of middle managers. When you make it to the top of your organization, you tend to shake things up by leading in an all together different style. Your real strength is in linking resources with the appropriate people in an almost uncanny way. You promote good will and friendship throughout the organization, and this trait allows you to bring even contentious parties together to act for the common good. A crisis is your chance to shine. As others bail out, you are just getting started.

How many of these traits apply to you?

__ You accept people as they are and do not try to change them

__ You make things happen by focusing on the here and now

__ You are at your best in contentious labor and management negotiations

__ You are an encouraging and positive reflection of your organization

__ Action and excitement follow you wherever you go

__ While you are one of the most practical of the sixteen types, you never forget the human side of the equation

__ You are fun loving, outgoing, and likeable

__ You are great at linking the appropriate person with the right resources

__ During crises, you have a great knack for easing tensions

__ You manage crises well

Words to Live By: pleasant, tolerant, cooperative, sociable, friendly, adaptable, enthusiastic, outgoing, talkative, easy-going, vivacious, and playful.

Jobs and Careers That Attract Your Type: Retail sales, news reporter, fund raiser, receptionist, labor relations mediator, team trainer, sports equipment sales, insurance agent, general contractor, interior decorator, home health care sales, special events coordinator, marine biologist, massage therapist, teacher, union organizer, transportation services, fire fighter, emergency medicine specialist, musician, producer, photographer, travel agent, social worker, home health specialist, child care provider, coach, alcohol and drug counselor, respiratory therapist, veterinarian, pharmacy technician, flight attendant, dietician, LPN, home health aid, emergency room nurse, and medical assistant.

Words You Use to Describe Yourself:_____

Extended Profile: Yours is perhaps the most sensual of the sixteen types. Don't get too excited now; the word is sensual, not sexual. You live in a world keenly aware of the senses that impact you. You are more aware of nature and human motivations than are many others, and you tend to pick up signals from those around you through what you see, feel, taste, smell, and hear.

These traits give you the reputation for being a good-natured realist ready to do whatever is necessary to make the relationship work, the contract succeed, or the task get done effectively. The fact that you can accomplish these things in a caring, laid back, and accepting way amazes others. For you, these traits are only natural.

Because your style is so open to input, so flexible, and at the same time unprejudiced and caring, you make a superb negotiator and mediator. All parties trust you to be open to their suggestions and points of view and to help them decide based on the facts that truly bear on the case. You have a knack for mediating without imposing your judgments on the case at hand.

What you are probably best known for at work is your spontaneity. You are unlikely to feel constrained by the rules and would much rather respond to what comes down the pike than plan out all twelve activities you expect to accomplish during the day. This may be a sticking point for the judgers you work with or for those who will expect greater precision in your plans. To the contrary, your best contribution comes when you are free to outline for yourself how you will go about your job. People of your temperament do not mind being told what their job is; you just do not want to be told how to do it. That rigid path saps all of your creativity and energy. You can be totally goal directed, as long as you have the chance to define the goals.

Because you tend to live life by the moment, you will be perceived as playing more than working. What you know is that real work won't get done unless you can play at the same time. Because most large bureaucratic organizations frown on such "playful" behavior, you probably have some outlet for your sensuous playfulness. It could be art, sports, ballet, race car driving, painting, landscaping, acting, or something much more idiosyncratic. You are, after all, a free spirit, and no one is going to tie you down to conventional behavior.

You are a real people person and revel in having others around you to add to the excitement. Not only do you enjoy working with people on teams, but you also love having others just drop by where you live. If you live with someone else, they better be prepared for constant socializing. People tend to just come and go when you are around. This flux appeals to you greatly.

You are a very generous person and will give of your self and your time graciously. Consequently, you are capable of being seduced easily into helping or volunteering your time to be with others. You enjoy making others happy, and sometimes you need to learn to just say "no."

Because you are so sympathetic to others' concerns, you do not enjoy being the bearer of bad news. Praising others comes easily to you; criticizing them does not. You prefer to sweep problems under the rug and hope they will go away. They will not. Wanting to be liked or appreciated can sometimes get in your way in your attempts to rise in the organization.

Type and Age: Although you have elected just four preferences as your "type," life is an ongoing experience of learning how to use all eight preferences at the appropriate time, for the appropriate task. You will develop different preferences at specific, predictable times in your life.

For your type, the flow is as follows:
  Dominant—extraverted Sensing (ages 8-15)
  Auxiliary—introverted Feeling (ages 16-30)
  Tertiary—extraverted Thinking (ages 31-40)
  Inferior—introverted iNtuition (ages 41-55)

What we refer to as your Dominant function is Sensing, which you express externally. To do your best work, you spend time gathering data in meetings and among others and in groups that you trust. Others you work with will hear you making requests for clear information. Your preference is to sort out all of this publicly, with the help of others. You probably developed this preference first, between the ages 8-15. When you judge and analyze the data, you use your Auxiliary function, which is Feeling. This function is expressed in the internal world; hence, you introvert it. You prefer quiet, alone time to consider the human dimension of your decision making process. It is easier for you to think about the impact on others or the values that are at stake when you are alone rather than in meetings. This function was likely developed between the ages of 16-30. Hence, by the end of college or beginning of your early professional years, the Sensing–Feeling ground floor to your personality has been laid. The middle two letters of your personality type become the team of preferences that you will trust the most into the beginning of midlife.

About the age of 31, one of your non-preferences asks to be dealt with. We call it your Tertiary function. For your type, it is Thinking judgments, which you extravert. Your best decision making, relative to objective analysis and cause and effect reasoning will be done publicly, in the external world. Others may even be surprised that you are reflecting on such concerns, but they will begin to be important to you during this period. From the ages of 31 to about 40 you will develop the capacity to deal more effectively with the logic involved. Your type does not change, but you learn how to use this non-preference when required. Your last preference to be developed we call the Inferior function. For you, it is iNtuition, which you introvert. During the ages of 41-55 you will become more comfortable thinking about ideas, visions, and possibilities, things that heretofore may have seemed extraneous, if not irrelevant, to you. When you use this function, you will do it in the internal world; hence, you introvert it.

Type, then, is far more than just 4 letters on a report form. If all goes well, and it rarely does, by late midlife, you will have developed the capacity to use each of the 8 preferences when needed, with some degree of sophistication. We call this process the full development of type.

Type Under Stress: Under heavy stress, you become rigid and arbitrary. Normally, when using your dominant function, which is extraverted Sensing, you are vivacious, precise, and realistic. You quickly see what needs attention and you get it done. When you suddenly get trapped working out of your inferior function, which is introverted iNtuition, everything changes. You become negative and pessimistic. Small things will bug you, and you will feel trapped in a maze and unable to extricate yourself. You will see the future in negative terms and obsess about its negative possibilities. Frightening images can plague you with self-doubt and you can fall into a spiral of frightening possibilities. Present and future possibilities get put on hold, as you obsess about the past. As a way out, you may turn to mystical ways of solving your problems or of understanding the universe.

Your Type and Ethics: You are often surprised by others who get worked up over abstract ethical principles or the need to legislate our moral behavior with some code of behavior. For you, what works is right. You are one of the most pragmatic of the sixteen types, and that pragmatism prevails over arbitrary rules. To be quite frank, you tend to be suspicious of those who try to establish core values for a company or legislate behavior at any level of our society. When a situation arises in which you have to decide right or wrong, you trust yourself to know what to do. All the codification of rules accomplishes is the creation of a system of sanctions by which others can second-guess your behavior. That seems stupid to you. Principles, values, ethics, and morality are all slippery and esoteric concepts for you. You just want to be accepted for who you are and judged by what you do. "Just do it," is the most important value in the workplace.

Other ESFP's That You Know_____

ENFP

Advocate, Energizer, Discoverer, Catalyst

Giving Life, You, and Ideas an Extra Squeeze

Overview: You have indicated that you prefer Extraversion, iNtuition, Feeling, and Perceiving as your favorite ways of dealing with the world around you. By selecting those preferences, you join about 5% of the world's population who share the same personality type.

Other High Performers who share your type include: Oprah Winfrey, William Jefferson Clinton, Snoopy, General Colin Powell, Julia Roberts, Will Rogers, Gerald Ford, Jesse Jackson, and former NYC Mayor Ed Koch.

Snapshot: The pursuit of endless possibilities energizes your life and the lives of those with whom you work and live. You are innovative and enthusiastic, and your versatile insights into the motivations of others, continuously amazes those who know you.

Leadership Style: In Fortune 500 Companies, your type comprises about 8.6 % of all presidents and CEO's, 2.4 % of senior and executive vice presidents, and 2.7 % of middle managers. Ideas run your world, and you love to launch projects and involve others in them. Your high levels of energy and enthusiasm excite others as well as sustain you when the going gets tough. Your style is to be innovative and insightful as you stay in constant pursuit of new possibilities.

How many of these traits apply to you?
___ You enjoy initiating change
___ Start up ventures excite you

___ You appreciate others and value their contributions

___ You tend to become the spokesperson for those who do not always have the power to speak for themselves

___ You enjoy being around creative and innovative people

___ Your personal enthusiasm is contagious

___ You tend to focus on possibilities as they influence lives and values

___ Your leadership style is infused with enthusiasm and energy

___ You listen well and pay attention to what motivates others

___ Those who work with you know that you will be tireless in involving and supporting them in all aspects of a project

Words to Live By: imaginative, perceptive, spontaneous, versatile, curious, creative, restless, energetic, friendly, expressive, open, and enthusiastic.

Jobs and Careers That Attract Your Type: Human resources management, mediator, publicist, consulting, psychology, diversity manager, translator, politics, newscaster, playwright, pastor, ombudsperson, social worker, nutritionist, strategic planner, international relations, advertising, marketing, social scientist, clergy, career counselor, teacher, child welfare counselor, restaurateur, retail sales, special education teacher, reporter, artist, public relations specialist, advertising, art director, speech pathologist, personal coach, journalist, actor, composer, and creative writer.

Words You Use to Describe Yourself:_____

Extended Profile: You are an innovative, high energy, caring instigator, always ready to help someone else or to explore an unknown horizon. You have heard these attributes before if you share these four letters. You have the knack of walking into a room and taking it immediately to a new level.

Because you have such a gift for communicating with others at several levels, you tend to be very persuasive, indeed seductive, in your ability to align others and build a consensus among people from diverse backgrounds and interests. You approach your work and life with enthusiasm. Your verve energizes others, and others energize you. It seems to be the perfect match. What frustrates you on the job and hurts you in relationships is when others do not reciprocate with the same degree of involvement, care, and affection.

While some get charged up by tackling a new problem and others get fixated on following procedures to the letter, you get energized by people. People and values form the heart of your life. You are, of all the sixteen types, the people person of all times. You tend to live, eat, sleep, and breathe people and values.

You enjoy hearing from others as well. Giving and receiving effective feedback in organizations is one of your real strengths. You, yourself know, that you really will not grow as a person unless you ask for and receive feedback from others on a routine basis. Remember former NYC Mayor, Ed Koch? "How am I doing? How am I doing?" was his persistent mantra. You would prefer to have positive feedback, but you will take whatever you can get. What is important is the feedback. That is the way you can improve and grow.

Because communication is your forte, you tend to speak well in front of groups and write even more persuasively.

You probably enjoy playing with language and the meanings of words, and can learn a foreign language the easiest of all the sixteen types. Indeed your facility with communication goes beyond verbal linguistics; you communicate with your entire body. From facial features to leg or foot position, you are aware of what you are doing all the time and have an incredible ability to communicate with nonverbals.

At the same time, this uncanny ability also allows you to "read" other people as well. If I am involved in labor-management negotiations, I want an ENFP on my side. You just have a knack for knowing what the other person is thinking—don't you?

I will walk out of a lecture to 500 people in an auditorium, and one of my ENFP consultants (by the way, I have several of them—ENFP's flock to the consulting business, the growing of people and teams) will let me know that there are 6 people on the right who aren't engaged and two on the left that feel left out. How does he know that? He is an ENFP, that's why. You just have that sense.

While you have this infectious ability to start projects and get others involved, you bore easily and sometimes have a problem finishing them. You just "kind of assume" that some J you are working with will take your ideas to conclusion. That behavior is often frustrating to those working with you. They have been excited by your ideas but left high and dry once your enthusiasm wears off.

In many ways you are an idealist. Oh, you will make claims to the contrary, and see yourself as a realist in many things, but beneath the surface lurks the notion that we could all be brothers and sisters if others simply had your understanding of values and saw the world as you did. For many of you, those brothers and sisters include whales, furry beasts of all kinds, laboratory animals, white spotted owls, snail darters, red wood trees, Palestinians, and IRA terrorists. Because you are a searcher after truth, you tend to see yourself as possessing it. "The Children of Light" who came and went as icons at the 2001 Winter Olympics in Salt Lake City, probably restored your faith in mankind.

Life, for those fortunate enough to be around you, stays exciting. Your enthusiasm sparks others into action as well. Even your leisure time tends to be filled with friends and activities. Reaching you at home by telephone on weekends is virtually impossible; you will be somewhere, doing something, with someone else. Helping out with family members, planting tulips with the homeowners association, attending civil organizations, playing tennis at the club, attending golf outings, coaching soccer, or sitting at Starbucks mentally solving the Mid East crisis or the stock market decline are all things that demand your immediate, undivided attention. You are busy, at least in your mind, all the time.

What sometimes goes missing because of all of your activities, are relationships. That is a real irony. While relationships are the cornerstone of your life, they often stay at the superficial level, because you are too busy "doing things." Others can read your signals as being open to intensifying the relationship, and they act accordingly. You are surprised and have to discourage them to back off. Their relationship was important to you, but so were twenty-four others. This behavior can make you a bit unpredictable as a spouse, lover, co-worker, parent, or friend. When others refer to you as fickle, you are surprised and a little hurt.

When you act as a mediator or group facilitator, you can

often encourage others to move far beyond that which they thought they were capable of doing. Because rank and status do not impress you, moving in and out of groups at every level of the organization comes easy to you. You will value the input from the production engineer as much as from the chief steward of the union or the CFO. Being naturally curious, you are open to hearing all sides of an issue before deciding. Hence, those you are working with will see you as an honest broker in attempting to arrive at any consensus.

Type and Age: Although you have elected just four preferences as your "type," life is an ongoing experience of learning how to use all eight preferences at the appropriate time, for the appropriate task. You will develop different preferences at specific, predictable times in your life.

For your type, the flow is as follows:

Dominant—extraverted iNtuition (ages 8-15)

Auxiliary—introverted Feeling (ages 16-30)

Tertiary—extraverted Thinking (ages 31-40)

Inferior—introverted Sensing (ages 41-55)

What we refer to as your Dominant function is iNtuition, which you express externally. The public world of theories, ideas, concepts, and possibilities excites and energizes you. You probably developed this preference first, between the ages 8-15. When you judge and analyze the data, you use your Auxiliary function, which is Feeling judgment. This function is expressed in the internal world; hence, you introvert it. You prefer quiet, alone time to come to closure on your ideas based on personal and value-centered considerations. This function was likely developed between the ages of 16-30. Hence, by the end of college or the beginning of your early professional years, the iNtuitive–Feeling ground floor to your personality has been laid. The middle two letters of your personality type become the team of preferences that you will trust the most into the beginning of midlife.

About the age of 31, one of your non-preferences asks to be dealt with. We call it your Tertiary function. For your type, it is Thinking judgment, which you extravert. When you logically analyze courses of action, you will do it publicly, in the external world. Others may even be surprised that you are reflecting on such concerns from a cause and effect relationship, but they will begin to be important to you during this period. From the ages of 31 to about 40 you will develop the capacity to do the logical analysis that has heretofore been unattractive to you. Your type does not change, but you learn how to use this non-preference when required. Your last preference to be developed we call the Inferior function. For you, it is Sensing, which you introvert. During the ages of 41-55 you will become more comfortable considering data, facts, and information. When you use this function, you will do it in the internal world; hence, you introvert it.

Type, then, is far more than just 4 letters on a report form. If all goes well, and it rarely does, by late midlife, you will have developed the capacity to use each of the 8 preferences when needed, with some degree of sophistication. We call this process the full development of type.

Type and Stress: Under heavy stress, you will become obsessed with irrelevant details and become overwhelmed by the plethora of data flooding into your world. Normally, when using your dominant function, which is extraverted iNtuition, you would simply ignore this onslaught from the sensory world. You would change models and live in the visionary world of the future. You would be quick to see new opportunities and direct your energies in that direction. You would tackle new projects with zeal and energy and amaze people with your vitality. When you suddenly get trapped working out of your inferior function, which is introverted Sensing, everything changes. You may gain weight as you over eat and over drink. You may get preoccupied with doing the unimportant and neglect those things most important to you. You acquire tunnel vision and get picky and cranky about small things, which you may escalate into grand issues. Eventually you may get run down physically by sleeping too little or exercising too much. Life is not fun for you or for those around you.

Your Type and Ethics: Values are very important to you. You see yourself as being incredibly value-centered. Indeed people and values are your focus. Let's admit, however, that values for you can be a little bit "gray," in the best sense of the term. The term situation ethics best describes your normal approach to valuing. Despite the rule or the principle that may have been violated, you may want to decide differently for each person involved depending on who is at stake or what values have been assailed. The value is invested in the person, not the abstract rule. This approach to ethical behavior can sometimes get you in hot water for seeming too soft or too fickle, in the eyes of others, when all the issues are surfaced. If that happens, so be it; for you, the human being is the most important consideration. Given the choice between justice and mercy, mercy usually gets your nod.

Other ENFP's That You Know_____

ENTP

Explorer, Challenger, Inventor, Generator
Inventive, Paradigm-Busting Entrepreneur

Overview: You have indicated that you prefer Extraversion, iNtuition, Thinking, and Perceiving as your favorite ways of dealing with the world around you. By selecting those preferences, you join about 5% of the world's population who share the same personality type.

Other High Performers who share your type include: Herb Kelleher (Southwest Airlines), Oscar Madison (The Odd Couple), John Foster Dulles, and Robin Williams.

Snapshot: Yours is one of the most entrepreneurial of the sixteen types. Your innovative and analytical approach to life attracts creative individuals and tends to worry those more traditionally minded. As one of the most individualistic of the sixteen types, you pride yourself on independence of thought and action.

Leadership Style: In Fortune 500 Companies, your type comprises 2.8 % of all presidents and CEO's, 7.2 % of senior and executive vice presidents, and 7.3 % of middle managers. You are one of the most entrepreneurial of the sixteen types. Your style is to be individualistic and iconoclastic. You get excited about leading new projects and like being on the cutting edge of technology and ideas. You are a catalyst for change and enjoy leading change processes begun by others. Risk taking comes naturally to you, and you tend to encourage others to act independently and take risks as necessary to improve the status quo.

How many of these traits apply to you?

___ You enjoy complex challenges—the bigger, the better

___ You enjoy freedom of action and the ability to act
    independently

___ You act as a catalyst to implement new systems

___ Your logic is compelling as you persuade others to
    embrace your position

___ In addressing organizational requirements, you enjoy a
    good complex system

___ Limitations and obstacles are simply problems to be
    overcome

___ Providing the new way to fix an old problem excites
    you

___ Versatility and innovation follow you wherever you go

___ You will take the initiative and encourage others to
    follow

___ Your leadership style encourages independence and
    freedom of action in others

Words to Live By: resourceful, theoretical, adaptive, analytical, strategic, independent, questioning, clever, challenging, creative, outspoken, and enterprising.

Jobs and Careers That Attract Your Type: Management
consulting, investment broker, systems design, research and
development, marketing, new business development, computer analyst, political scientist, politician, international
sales, journalism, actor, entrepreneur, dot com start-up ventures, talk show host, producer, art director, high school
teacher, financial planning, cardiology, public relations specialist, graphics designer, and attorney.

Words You Use to Describe Yourself:_____

Extended Profile: Your type, more so than any of the

other fifteen, is a whirlwind of ideas and possibilities. You move from scheme to scheme with so much ease and resiliency that you can leave others breathless in the process. You are a born entrepreneur, and whether it is a new product which you have been asked to launch, a joint venture the company wants you to bring together, or a new business you decide to launch on your own, you will tackle whatever obstacles stand in your way with enthusiasm and creativity.

As long as the project lies in front of you, you stay excited because you prefer to live in the realm of the possible. Once the gears begin to turn, the joint venture has taken off, or the aircraft rolls out of the hanger, your interests in the project begin to wane. You sometimes have to fight to keep interested. Beginnings fascinate you. Middles are sustainable, but once the end is in view....

While you are a tough taskmaster with others, you are even tougher on yourself. Learning of all kinds has probably fascinated you since your youth. Your interests may take you into disciplines seemingly as disparate as politics, engineering, sports trivia, classical music, and quantum physics. If you read Thomas Pynchon, you do it more for his use of the theory of entropy than you do for his literary aesthetics. You drive yourself to ever-higher levels of performance and drive others there as well; however, if the truth be known, you probably really don't think others are up to the task. In dealing with others, particularly those to whom you report, you have to guard yourself against coming across as intellectually arrogant.

You make a tough parent as well. When your teenage son brings home a report card with five A's and a B, you know the first question you are going to ask, don't you. You probably don't even stop first to congratulate him on the five A's. After all, you wouldn't need others to tell you to improve, you would be lacing into yourself already. You are your own best critic and too often others' as well.

Although you have tremendous interpersonal skills, you often have not developed the social mask to include the niceties that others may need. People are naturally attracted to you because of your ideas and energy, but without the occasional pat on the back, a sincere thank-you, or "How's everything?" that comes naturally to others, you may lose their loyalty and respect.

Finding just the right organization to work for is critical for your type. You are independent as a worker and even more independent as a thinker. If you get trapped in a job that demands a routine approach to business, you will quickly lose interest and fly the coup. You need to see your impact each day on the job. If someone asks you to be just a small cog on the wheel, they will be quickly surprised to find that you are really the fly in the ointment, just to have a little fun.

On the surface, you may appear to others as flexible and sometimes flighty. Beneath the surface, however, you are focused and few people work harder, as long as you have a say in the direction of the work. Once you have found the quintessential idea, the unique marketing factor, or the new drug discovery, you will become a downright workaholic to bring the idea to fruition.

Type and Age: Although you have elected just four preferences as your "type," life is an ongoing experience of learning how to use all eight preferences at the appropriate time, for the appropriate task. You will develop different preferences at specific, predictable times in your life.

For your type, the flow is as follows:

Dominant—extraverted iNtuition (ages 8-15)
Auxiliary—introverted Thinking (ages 16-30)
Tertiary—extraverted Feeling (ages 31-40)
Inferior—introverted Sensing (ages 41-55)

What we refer to as your Dominant function, is iNtuition, which you express externally. To do your best work, you generate ideas and possibilities easier than any of the other types. Your preference is to share these creative notions publicly, with others. You probably developed this preference first, between the ages 8-15. When you judge and analyze the data, you use your Auxiliary function, which is Thinking judgment. This function is expressed in the internal world; hence, you introvert it. You prefer quiet, alone time to perform your best, logical analysis. This function was likely developed between the ages of 16-30. Hence, by the end of college or beginning of your early professional years, the iNtuitive–Thinking ground floor to your personality has been laid. The middle two letters of your personality type become the team of preferences that you will trust the most into the beginning of midlife.

About the age of 31, one of your non-preferences asks to be dealt with. We call it your Tertiary function. For your type, it is Feeling judgment, which you extravert. When you do your decision making, relative to personal, value-related concerns, it will be done publicly, in the external world. Others may even be surprised that you are reflecting on such concerns, but they will begin to be important to you during this period. From the ages of 31 to about 40 you will develop the capacity to empathize. Your type does not change, but you learn how to use this non-preference when required. Your last preference to be developed we call the Inferior function. For you, it is Sensing, which you introvert. During the ages of 41-55 you will become more comfortable spending time looking at data and facts that may have a bearing on your work, things which heretofore may have seemed extraneous, if not irrelevant, to you. When you use this function, you will do it in the internal world; hence, you introvert it.

Type, then, is far more than just 4 letters on a report form. If all goes well, and it rarely does, by late midlife, you will have developed the capacity to use each of the 8 preferences when needed, with some degree of sophistication. We call this process the full development of type.

Type Under Stress: Under heavy stress, you tend to become preoccupied with unimportant things and obsess about them. Normally, when using your dominant function, which is extraverted iNtuition, you are energetic and creative in responding to changing circumstances. You take on all comers and show real ingenuity when confronted by seemingly impossible odds. When you suddenly get trapped working out of your inferior function, which is introverted Sensing, everything changes. You have a hard time doing anything because you are too overwhelmed by the influx of data. Energy yields to paralysis and the phrase getting trapped by "analysis paralysis" was coined to describe you. During these times, you feel isolated and alone. Feelings of despair and sadness pervade your efforts. You can feel numb and unloved. At worst, this can cause you to neglect your own health and you may eventually become ill.

Your Type and Ethics: Your approach to deciding what ethical behavior encompasses often surprises others. Values are incredibly important to you, and you often make that fact clear to others who live and work with you; however, values mean something altogether different to you than to other types. The persons involved or the rules that are broken are mostly irrelevant to you. What is important is the principle at stake, beneath the rules. In fact, you may be willing to break any rule or law that exists, as long as there is a clearer principle at stake behind the rule. Indeed, you may see the rules as merely arbitrary impediments to ethical behavior. You are willing to challenge them just as you would challenge any other arbitrary system. Once the principle at stake is clear, so is your necessary action. With ethics, as with most things in this life, you will seem antiauthoritarian and self-willed. For you, that is just fine.

Other ENTP's That You Know_____

ESTJ

Supervisor, Manager, Administrator, Implementer

Responsible Pillar of Society

Overview: You have indicated that you prefer Extraversion, Sensing, Thinking, and Judging as your favorite ways of dealing with the world around you. By selecting those preferences, you join about 13% of the world's population who share the same personality type.

Other High Performers who share your type include: Barbara Bush, General Norman Schwartzkopf, Lucy Van Pelt (Peanuts comic strip), Archie Bunker, Angela Pickles (Rugrats cartoon series), Giv'em Hell Harry Truman, and Joan Rivers.

Snapshot: You are decisive and tough-minded. You prefer to organize operations and systems well in advance and then take charge and work logically to ensure mission success. Logical analysis is your path to success.

Leadership Style: Your type is one of the four that rises most naturally to the leadership of large and complex organizations. In Fortune 500 Companies, your type comprises 5.7 % of presidents and CEO's, 17.6 % of senior and executive vice presidents, and 18.8 % of middle managers. You act quickly and decisively to organize materials and people for the successful completion of a project. You are a natural manager and are very comfortable taking charge of projects. The larger the project, the more comfortable you are being in charge. Rules, procedures, and policies are all helpful to you, and you are comfortable working within their context. Traditions are also important to you, and you value the history of the organization as a way of understanding your roles and responsibilities in the present.

How many of these traits apply to you?

__ You follow through diligently step-by-step

__ You are quicker than most to decide

__ You get to the heart of the matter quickly

__ You seek leadership opportunities

__ You easily see flaws in advance

__ You like to organize events and people

__ If others work for you, you will monitor their activities

__ You enjoy applying past experiences to current problems

__ You take charge quickly and happily

__ You tend to critique others and processes logically

Words to Live By: responsible, conscientious, direct, organized, objective, decisive, logical, systematic, structured, impersonal, practical, and efficient.

Jobs and Careers That Attract Your Type: Retail sales, medicine, business management, military, government service, teaching, trades, corrections officer, police, firemen, factory supervisor, credit manager, purchasing agent, physician, judge, engineering (mechanical, industrial, metallurgical, electrical), finance, project management, dentist, general contractor, farmer, auditor, banking, insurance agent, security guard, pharmaceutical sales, corrections officer, stockbroker, and paralegal.

Words You Use to Describe Yourself＿＿＿＿＿＿＿＿＿

Extended Profile: Of all the sixteen types, yours is one of the most traditional of the combinations of sensing and judging. You have a very clear cut set of rights and wrongs and shoulds and oughts that guide your behavior and should, in your opinion, guide that of others as well. Your sense of personal responsibility and obligation is the background of our culture and of every responsible large and complex organization that thrives in it.

You are a charming traditionalist. This sense of tradition pervades your view of organizations and of the family. Let's start with the family. There should be one dad and one wife. Traditionally these two should be of different genders. These two should have children and rear them on the basis of traditional values. While both parents are important for the raising of children, if one decides to stay home to raise them, it should be the mom. Without pushing this model too far, you get the picture. The model that has worked so long will continue to work. These two parents should stay together forever, by the way. That was the intent of the original contract. If one chooses to violate that contract, that person is irresponsible, and it may take you a long time to forgive them.

When there are holidays, there are certain traditions that should be followed year in and year out. You will invest real sentiment in certain decorations that you hang each year. If there are special figurines you put out for Christmas, Chanukah, Halloween, or the Fourth of July, they probably always go in the same place. It just makes you feel good. Celebrations, family reunions, and holiday gatherings are very important to you.

Similarly, there should be a clear hierarchy in organizations. When all employees know their roles and responsibilities and to whom they report, everything runs much more efficiently. It just seems reasonable to you that if there are rules, they should be followed.

For these reasons, you make an outstanding supervisor and manager. Yours is one of four types most likely to rise to the top of major corporations. We trust you for the sense of responsibility you bring to the workplace. Because there is a clear-cut set of rights and wrongs for you, your word is your bond. When you shake hands, the deal is done. Not only do you do well when you are in charge, but you also enjoy it. The roles of commander, skipper, executive, and business manager appeal to you much more than subaltern, assistant, aide, or intern. This position gives you the chance to plot out the entire scheme of things, plan the entire attack, or develop the entire business strategy. This position at the helm is your cup of tea.

Should you have to reprimand an employee or even fire them, you have a much easier job doing it than one of your empathist colleagues. You do not enjoy doing it any more than anyone else, but by golly, the rules are the rules! If someone does not live up to expectations, they should pay the piper.

Having a predictable work and business life appeals to you greatly. On the job you are frugal and get angry when you see others cutting the corners, wasting supplies, or sitting down on their shift. Being naturally conservative, you tend to save in traditional ways. Preparing for the future by saving, having Roth IRA's, and buying savings bonds is the way to go. Having high credit card debt strikes you as irresponsible, and when you sometimes have to run up charges during tough times, you fret about it to no end. You would much rather skimp and save today, in order to enjoy a comfortable future. When you invest in personal possessions, you prefer to buy high quality ones and take good care of them.

If you own a car, and the maintenance guide calls for check-ups at 5,000, 10,000, 25,000, and 35,000 miles, you will be in line to drop the car off at the dealer to take care of it. If the manual suggests oil changes at every 6,000 miles, you probably do it every 5,000 just to make sure.

We can count on you to be the provider. As a supervisor, you will protect your people. As a parent, you will provide for the family and plan systematically for your retirement. You like to feel responsible for others and have a strong sense of responsibility.

Whereas some prefer the chase or the process, you prefer the capture or the product. When given a task, you work to get it done. If someone gives you a general mission to accomplish you are excited about being given the responsibility, but you are not comfortable until you break it down into the various tasks that must be accomplished and have specific people assigned to accomplish each task.

Type and Age: Although you have elected just four preferences as your "type," life is an ongoing experience of learning how to use all eight preferences at the appropriate time, for the appropriate task. You will develop different preferences at specific, predictable times in your life.

For your type, the flow is as follows:
Dominant—extraverted Thinking (ages 8-15)
Auxiliary—introverted Sensing (ages 16-30)
Tertiary—extraverted iNtuition (ages 31-40)
Inferior—introverted Feeling (ages 41-55)

What we refer to as your Dominant function, is Thinking judgment, which you express externally. When you speak, you give us answers, decisions, and finality. You sound decisive and probably are. You probably developed this preference first, between the ages 8-15. Before you arrive at your decisions, you have spent time gathering all of the data and facts you think are necessary to decide appropriately. You express this function, however, in the internal world; hence, you introvert it, and we do not know you have done it. You prefer quiet, alone time to lay the basis for your decisions. This function was likely developed between the ages of 16-30. Hence, by the end of college or beginning of your early professional years, the Thinking–Sensing ground floor to your personality has been laid. The middle two letters of your personality type become the team of preferences that you will trust the most into the beginning of midlife.

About the age of 31, one of your non-preferences asks to be dealt with. We call it your Tertiary function. For your type, it is iNtuition, which you extravert. When you explore ideas and generate possibilities you will do it publicly, in the external world. Others may even be surprised that you are reflecting on such concerns, but they will begin to be important to you during this period. From the ages of 31 to about 40 you will develop this desire to think more broadly in the world of ideas. Your type does not change, but you learn how to use this non-preference when required. Your last preference to be developed we call the Inferior function. For you, it is Feeling judgment, which you introvert. During the ages of 41-55 you will begin asking more value-centered, interpersonal kinds of questions which, heretofore, may have seemed extraneous, if not irrelevant to you. When you use this function, you will do it in the internal world; hence, you introvert it.

Type, then, is far more than just 4 letters on a report form. If all goes well, and it rarely does, by late midlife, you will have developed the capacity to use each of the 8 preferences when needed, with some degree of sophistication. We call this process the full development of type.

Type Under Stress: Under heavy stress, you may become overly emotional and seem flighty. Normally, when using your dominant function, which is extraverted Thinking judgment, you are a clear and lucid analyst. You are consistent, firm, and just, and expect others to be as well. When you get trapped using your inferior function, which is introverted Feeling judgment, everything changes. Any suggestions you receive, you are likely to take as attacks or insults. Rather than acting, you are likely to pout and find fault with others. When you try to deal with your stress, you may yell, cry, or show other emotional outbursts. You don't like yourself, and others are confused by your "over-reaction." Feeling like a victim is new to you, and you can occasionally "shut down" or play the martyr. At work you wear a good professional mask, and others with whom you work are not aware you are experiencing uncertainties, but internally you worry about losing control publicly. At worst, you may put up a strong front at work then sob uncontrollably and yell at other drivers all the way home, while you are alone in the car.

Your Type and Ethics: Your type is one of four, for whom values are crystal clear. If someone wants to know what is right or wrong, you can find it written down somewhere, in black and white. You will gladly take us to volume III, page 26 and show us rules one through fifteen. You will follow them. We should too. The rules have the status of laws, and ethical people should be expected to agree upon their meaning and follow them. You are quite suspicious of those who might flaunt the rules and see such individuals as reckless. Likewise, those who might want to decide differently, depending on the situation, strike you as flaky and irresponsible. You have little sympathy for those who violate the established values and want to have them punished for their transgressions. The rules are there for our mutual good, and a mood of righteous indignation often pervades your sense of required justice.

Other ESTJ's That You Know_____

ESFJ
Facilitator, Teacher, Seller, Caretaker
Gracious Host and Hostess of the World

Overview: You have indicated that you prefer Extraversion, Sensing, Feeling, and Judging as your favorite ways of dealing with the world around you. By selecting those preferences, you join about 13% of the world's population who share the same personality type.

Other High Performers who share your type include: Dwight David Eisenhower, Santa Claus, George Bush (43), Isiah Thomas, Felix Unger (The Odd Couple), Sean Hanidy (talk show host), and Tiger Woods.

Snapshot: Your type is one of the most generous of the sixteen types with your time and energy. You are tactful and compassionate, and you strive to create sound relationships with those with whom you work. Order, and routine help you to create harmonious human interactions.

Leadership Style: In Fortune 500 Companies, your type comprises less than 1 % of presidents and CEO's, about 1.5 % of senior and executive vice presidents, and 2.8 % of middle managers. You are a gracious individual and lead with élan and confidence. You often surprise others by your ability to see through pretense and to win over others who have vastly different points of view. Hard work comes easily to you, and you set the example for others to follow. You focus on the immediate goals and get the job done with class and immediacy. Traditions are important to you, and you enjoy participating in all the rites attending them. In all things honor and integrity are core, and your word is your bond.

How many of these traits apply to you?

___ You enjoy team work

___ You are careful to pay attention to others' needs and desires

___ Upholding the traditions of the country, the organization, and the family are important to you

___ You keep those working with you on a project well informed

___ You respect the rules and the norms and expect others to as well

___ Hard work and follow-through are what you expect

___ Completing a task in a timely way and being rewarded for it are pleasurable

___ You are quite comfortable handling routine matters

___ In working with others, you are tactful and diplomatic

___ You lead though personal example, and gain good will from those who work with you by never asking them to do anything you, yourself, would not do. You are a model of ethical behavior

Words to Live By: conscientious, friendly, caring, responsive, traditional, harmonious, tactful, loyal, personable, diplomatic, thorough, cooperative, responsible, fastidious, and sociable.

Jobs and Careers That Attract Your Type: Politician, teacher, human resources professional, religious educator, special forces soldier, veterinarian, professional athlete, social worker, military officer, physician, nurse, special education teacher, international retail sales person, receptionist, telemarketer, paralegal, counselor, minister, rabbi, priest, personal banker, office manager, interior decorator, credit counselor, retail shop owner, marriage counselor, couples mediator, LPN, RN, optometrist, drill sergeant, optician, dentist, athletic coach, and insurance agent.

Words You Use to Describe Yourself:_____

Extended Profile: Wanted, a talented, caring, people-centered, out-going individual, who is willing to go the extra mile for colleagues and customers alike. If you see that advertisement, jump on it, because what they are looking for is a person with your cardinal virtues. You will excel in any profession that gives you the chance to work closely with people every day. You are outgoing and generous in all of your dealings.

Of all the sixteen personality types, yours is the most friendly, warm, and personable. You enjoy working in a harmonious work place and you will foster that harmony wherever you go. Your values and beliefs are very important to you, and from your standpoint they are absolute and unwavering. Given a chance, you want to pass those same values on to your employees and family.

That family is very important to you. You believe the home should be a place of harmony and peace. You expect your house to be your castle. Parents should be in charge, and children should be respectful to the parents. Everything has a place, and you are most at ease when things are orderly and neat. To some extent, your home and your clothing are an extension of yourself. You pride yourself on being both neat and classy. To that end, you like having nice things and will work hard to afford well-made, stylish clothing and a house that is just a bit extravagant. Inside you have decorated it with taste and a bit of elegance that is an extension of your own personality.

In the ongoing choice between justice and mercy, you fall squarely on the justice side. The clear sense of right and wrong that informs your worldview helps you to feel armed with moral rectitude when you are called upon to censure others. As a child you probably even sent yourself to your room from time to time, if you knew that you had crossed the boundary. Your code is very clear, and you will insist that those who work and live with you follow it as well. When others do not work as diligently as you, treat children or other innocents badly, or seem to flaunt the values of the family or organization, you tend to have a strong sense of righteous indignation. You want to see them punished and expect those who are in charge, to make sure that justice is carried out swiftly.

In all of your relationships, you are thoughtful and unselfish, sympathetic and tactful. When competition occurs, it is not unusual for you to support the underdog. Even when your team wins, there is that shadow that crosses in front of your sun, making you wonder how the loser feels.

Service professions appeal to your type greatly. Early in your life you probably thought about careers in the military, medicine, teaching, or the ministry. Because of your delightful approach to work and others, the world is your apple. Just be careful always to choose a profession that lets you influence others.

The very high expectations you have for yourself can sometimes pose a double whammy for you. You know you have incredible potential, but sometimes you fail temporarily to live up to your own expectations. You can get down on yourself and even become depressed from time to time for performing to the level that others would be excited to reach.

Because you want peace and harmony where you live and work, you can sometimes wax Quixotic, despite your sensing roots. You may find yourself tilting at windmills that no one else cares about. Because you like neatness, and because you are generous to a fault with your time and energy, you may even want to do others' work, clean others' offices and rooms to help them out, only to find they resent your efforts and see it as an intrusion on their space. And here, you were just trying to help!

You like being immersed in the real world, and when you read, you probably enjoy biographies of real people. When you listen to stories, you like them to be authentic and rooted in reality, so you can create pictures in your mind to go along with them.

As a conversationalist, you astound people even at an early age with your perspicacity, wit, and vocabulary. When others speak to you, you sound wise beyond your years. As you get older, others will love to listen to you as you spin your yarns about events that happened to you. You usually have a way of painting vivid word pictures, selecting just the perfect $ 2.00 word. You also have a knack for remembering details with uncanny accuracy and may become a trivia nut for historical or sports facts.

Change does not excite you. Familiar patterns are comfortable, and you may see rapid changes as irresponsible. After all, there are all those traditions to think about. Particularly at holiday time, you can get pretty emotional about all those special knick-knacks that you unwrap from the attic year after year. They are more of those special possessions that you value so much.

When you are in a leadership role, you feel a strong sense of loyalty to your colleagues or teammates. Earning and sustaining their allegiance are important to you, and you place a high premium on organizational values and esprit de corps. You will work hard to ensure that each person is in just the right job and knows her or his role with precision. Once that is all worked out, all of you will follow the rules, because the "rules are our friends."

Results are important to you. If you are given a job to do, you will work diligently until it is complete. Indeed, you will tend to work longer without a break and harder than most of your friends. All you need is a compliment from time to time to keep you going. After the job is done, you are ready to play—not before.

Because building relationships comes so easy to you, yours is one of two types that are most successful working in Latin America and Asia. In those two parts of the world, the relationship is primary, even before you discuss the technical merits of the product. You feel that way instinctively and create the kind of business atmosphere most likely to be successful.

Type and Age: Although you have elected just four preferences as your "type," life is an ongoing experience of learning how to use all eight preferences at the appropriate time, for the appropriate task. You will develop different preferences at specific, predictable times in your life.

For your type, the flow is as follows:
Dominant—extraverted Feeling (ages 8-15)
Auxiliary—introverted Sensing (ages 16-30)
Tertiary—extraverted iNtuition (ages 31-40)
Inferior—introverted Thinking (ages 41-55)

What we refer to as your Dominant function, is Feeling judgment, which you express externally. When you speak, others will hear your concerns and decisions based on the values and people involved. They come first in your life, and you decide accordingly. You probably developed this preference first, between the ages 8-15. When you arrive at your decisions, you base them on all the appropriate data and information available to you. It is the factual approach to understanding the events, which is most important. When you do this, you use your Auxiliary function, which is Sensing. This function is expressed in the internal world; hence, you introvert it. You prefer quiet, alone time to do your best data gathering or assaying of the samples. This function was likely developed between the ages of 16-30. Hence, by the end of college or beginning of your early professional years, the Feeling–Sensing ground floor to your personality has been laid. The middle two letters of your personality type become the team of preferences that you will trust the most into the beginning of midlife.

About the age of 31, one of your non-preferences asks to be dealt with. We call it your Tertiary function. For your type, it is iNtuition, which you extravert. When you brainstorm and consider alternative models, you will do it publicly, in the external world. Others may even be surprised that you are reflecting on such concerns, but they will begin to be important to you during this period. From the ages of 31 to about 40 you will develop this capacity to move more easily in the world of theories, concepts, and possibilities. Your type does not change, but you learn how to use this non-preference when required. Your last preference to be developed we call the Inferior function. For you, it is Thinking judgment, which you introvert. During the ages of 41-55 you will become more comfortable making decisions based on logic and the cause and effect reasoning involved than you have in the past. When you use this function, you will do it in the internal world; hence, you introvert it.

Type, then, is far more than just 4 letters on a report form.

If all goes well, and it rarely does, by late midlife, you will have developed the capacity to use each of the 8 preferences when needed, with some degree of sophistication. We call this process the full development of type.

Type Under Stress: Under heavy stress, you tend to stop listening and seem "deaf" to others' suggestions. Normally, when using your dominant function, which is extraverted Feeling, you are caring, polite, and nurturing. You stay very attentive to others' needs and work creatively with them to solve problems and work out differences. When you suddenly get trapped working out of your inferior function, which is introverted Thinking, everything changes. Empathy turns to criticism. You can find little good in what others do. Even your humor may turn deprecatory. You can be almost universal in your condemnation of others. They become impediments to your success rather than teammates or colleagues. Rather than working with others, you tend to see them as opponents with which to do battle. Others will see you as overly domineering, not helpful or collaborative. Increasingly depressed, you begin to withdraw and feel inadequate to deal with life. The search for answers to your way out may lead you to some absolute remedy in the form of religion or philosophy which you apply universally.

Your Type and Ethics: Your type is one of four, for whom values are crystal clear. If someone wants to know what is right or wrong, you can find it written down somewhere, in black and white. You will gladly take us to volume III, page 26 and show us rules one through fifteen. You will follow them. We should too. The rules have the status of laws, and ethical people should be expected to agree upon their meaning and follow them. You are quite suspicious of those who might flaunt the rules and see such individuals as reckless. Likewise, those who might want to decide differently, depending on the situation, strike you as flaky and irresponsible. You have little sympathy for those who violate the established values and want to have them punished for their transgressions. The rules are there for our mutual good, and a mood of righteous indignation often pervades your sense of required justice.

Other ESFJ's That You Know_____

ENFJ
Envisioner, Persuader, Mentor, Ally
Charismatic, Empathic Architect of Ideals

Overview: You have indicated that you prefer Extraversion, iNtuition, Feeling, and Judging as your favorite ways of dealing with the world around you. By selecting those preferences, you join about 5% of the world's population who share the same personality type.

Other High Performers who share your type include: Ronald Reagan, Martin Luther King Jr., Mikhail Gorbachev, Rev. Billy Graham, Jim Jones, Vladimir Putin, José Maria Fugueres (President of Costa Rica), Carlos Menem (former President of Argentina), Adolph Hitler, and Rev. Jerry Falwell.

Snapshot: Yours is probably the most charismatic of all the sixteen types. You have a keen understanding of others' motivations and use those insights to facilitate effective team and interpersonal communications. Tolerance and respect for others are hallmarks of you approach to life.

Leadership Style: In Fortune 500 Companies, your type comprises 5.7 % of presidents and CEO's, 1.1 % of senior and executive vice presidents, and 1.6 % of middle managers. You are a natural motivator of others and easily attract others to join you in a cause. Your style is enthusiastic and appealing, and other people simply enjoy being around you. You are interpersonally adept, and you stay focused on your coworkers' or followers' needs. When leading an organization, you will be sure to challenge it to set clear values and to live up to them on a daily basis. Values are there to impact decisions not just to impress customers and suppliers.

How many of these traits apply to you?
__ You enjoy and encourage cooperation from others
__ You not only enjoy, but inspire, meaningful change
__ You constantly challenge your organization to live up to its stated values
__ When managing others, you are an active participant, not a passive observer
__ Bringing a project to a successful conclusion pleases you
__ Encouraging others to take risks to become great comes naturally to you
__ You enjoy being the one to communicate the organization's values
__ You are the natural spokesperson for a team or project
__ You are truly adept at understanding others
__ Your personal enthusiasm and magnetism enrich others' lives

Words to Live By: congenial, concerned, energetic, expressive, verbal, idealistic, supportive, diplomatic, enthusiastic, responsible, personable, and loyal.

Jobs and Careers that Attract Your Type: Advertising, marketing, consulting, clergy, social worker, dean of students, alcohol and drug counselor, outplacement counselor, head hunter, entertainer, editor, sales manager, journalist, politician, talk show host, facilitator, speech therapist, psychologist, recreational director, recruiter, sales trainer, travel agent, graphics designer, TV producer, fund raiser, director of communications, artist, translator, and career counselor.

Words You Use to Describe Yourself:_____

Extended Profile: Charisma and communication character-ize the heart of your style. Because you are perhaps the most charismatic of all the sixteen types, you have an envi-able knack for being able to marshal large numbers of peo-ple in support of a cause. That cause might be a political movement, a corporate vision statement, a religious tenet, a community activity, a protest, or a crackpot notion. Because of that power, your moral purpose always has to be clear. Cool Aid, after all, comes in many varieties.

Once you have a message to communicate, you have no hesitancy in letting others know what you believe. Although you can write well, your greatest strength comes from oral communication. It is not unusual to find you making presentations to the Wall Street analysts, con-sulting with heads of state, appearing on the Oprah Show as her shrink of the day, or speaking to a sales conference. When you consult it is usually in the areas of personal and media communication. Many of your type find their way into managerial and executive coaching, because of your ability to influence others.

Relationships are critical to your personal life, and you are more than happy to go the extra mile to foster strong ties with another person. Being so interpersonally savvy, you know how to say just the right thing to persuade others to agree with you. Sometimes you can try so hard to say and do the right thing that you can find yourself conforming to others' expectations, rather than maintaining your own vision. Approval from others is very important to you. If you fail to achieve it, the defeat can sometimes be crush-ing to you.

If you work for someone you admire, you can sometimes be seduced into following him or her to Abilene. If you like that person, you may tend to like everything he or she proposes. Similarly, if you dislike the person in charge, you can sometimes argue against every proposal, regardless of how sound it might be. Authority, for you, rests in the person, and your type sometimes has a hard time separating the person from the process.

In a similar vein, because pleasing other people is a very important issue for you, if someone criticizes your work, you may take it as a personal attack. The person speaking to you may like you immensely but disapprove only of something you have done. Separating the two, again, is hard for people with your preferences. More so than most people, you will tend to personalize all such comments as ad hominem attacks. Because it is hard for you to hear any criticism as other than a personal attack, it is sometimes difficult for your type to learn from your mistakes objectively. You may have never considered the criticism seriously enough.

The world is your oyster in terms of professions and interests. Your perspicacity and verve help you to stay attentive to possibilities for yourself and others. You may change careers many times in search of the job that fits you just right. What they will all have in common is a platform from which you can help others or improve their communication of a message. In that regard, you often help others find their appropriate niche as well. You can recognize talents in others, which they themselves may not be aware of yet, and goad them into pursuing new options and possibilities. Your antennae are always out, scanning the environment for the many possibilities that engulf us.

One of your real gifts is the ability to talk to anyone, anytime. When you walk into a meeting or sit down at the table, your style, body language, smile, and what Grandma used to call your "gift for gab" immediately make you the center of attraction. As an empathist, you understand how to approach each person differently and how to appeal to what they need to feel included. It is a marvelous gift that assists you in forming teams and consensus much more quickly than most.

This same ability to understand people has its flip side for you, as well. People will use your shoulder to cry on with startling regularity. Wherever you work and whatever your job, people in your organization will seek you out to ask your advice. You tend to get sucked in to the emotional lives of many people, and this connection may cause you to pay a heavy emotional tax. Others can simply burn you out after a while, and you have a very hard time just saying "no." Sadly, when you do manage to escape from others' concerns, you will feel guilty for having abandoned them.

You are an idealist, and that idealism pervades every aspect of your life. If you are in a relationship, you will tend to idealize it. There is no way anyone can live up to an ideal posture. Those fortunate enough to have you for a friend know that you will always be loyal. They may not hear from you for ten years, but if you can reconnect, it will be as though you have never been apart.

Type and Age: Although you have elected just four preferences as your "type," life is an ongoing experience of learning how to use all eight preferences at the appropriate time, for the appropriate task. You will develop different preferences at specific, predictable times in your life.

For your type, the flow is as follows:
   Dominant—extraverted Feeling (ages 8-15)
   Auxiliary—introverted iNtuition (ages 16-30)
   Tertiary—extraverted Sensing (ages 31-40)
   Inferior—introverted Thinking (ages 41-55)

What we refer to as your Dominant function, is Feeling judgment, which you express externally. Your strength lies in the judgments you arrive at based on value-centered, personal considerations. People and values are in the forefront of your decision making process, and you share those decisions with others; hence, you extravert them. You probably developed this preference first, between the ages 8-15. As you arrive at these decisions, you do so on the basis of ideas, models, and theories. You use your Auxiliary function, which is iNtuition. This function is expressed in the internal world; hence, you introvert it. You prefer quiet, alone time to generate ideas, consider all the possibilities at stake, and regenerate your energy. This function was likely developed between the ages of 16-30. Hence, by the end of college or beginning of your early professional years, the Feeling–iNtuitive ground floor to your personality has been laid. The middle two letters of your personality type become the team of preferences that you will trust the most into the beginning of midlife.

About the age of 31, one of your non-preferences asks to be dealt with. We call it your Tertiary function. For your type, it is Sensing, which you extravert. When you begin to look at the pertinent data or facts that may be important to you, you will do it publicly, in the external world. Others may even be surprised that you are reflecting on such concerns, but they will begin to be important to you during this period. From the ages of 31 to about 40 you will develop this interest in specificity. Your type does not change, but you learn how to use this non-preference when required. Your last preference to be developed we call the Inferior function. For you, it is Thinking judgment, which you introvert. During the ages of 41-55 you will become more comfortable deciding based on logic and impersonal reasoning rather than just the impact on people. These are things, which heretofore may have seemed extraneous, if not irrelevant to you. When you use this function, you will do it in the internal world; hence, you introvert it.

Type, then, is far more than just 4 letters on a report form. If all goes well, and it rarely does, by late midlife, you will have developed the capacity to use each of the 8 preferences when needed, with some degree of sophistication. We call this process the full development of type.

Type Under Stress: Under heavy stress, your type can become carping and argumentative. Normally, when using your dominant function, which is extraverted Feeling, you are a creative and caring individual. Others are attracted to you for your creativity and passion. When you suddenly get trapped working out of your inferior function, which is introverted Thinking, everything changes. Your passion gets sapped and you want to cash in your chips. Those around you can do no right and you become critical of virtually everything. If you are in charge, you tend to act in a pig-headed way and take input from no one. Your values, which normally "run your ship" get shipwrecked and may get you in trouble. You might turn to an expert for the way out of your dilemma. Sometimes the expert is a therapist, a priest, a guru, or a self-help book. Sometimes you make a wholesale midlife correction and choose a new career. You begin to cherish quiet, reflective time to think through changes you need to make in your life.

Your Type and Ethics: Values are very important to you. You see yourself as being incredibly value-centered. Indeed people and values are your focus. Let's admit, however, that values for you can be a little bit "gray," in the best sense of the term. The term situation ethics best describes your normal approach to valuing. Despite the rule or the principle that may have been violated, you may want to decide differently for each person involved depending on who is at stake or what values have been assailed. The value is invested in the person, not the abstract rule. This approach to ethical behavior can sometimes get you in hot water for seeming too soft or too fickle, in the eyes of others, when all the issues are surfaced. If that happens, so be it; for you, the human being is the most important consideration. Given the choice between justice and mercy, mercy usually gets your nod.

Other ENFJ's That You Know

ENTJ
Strategist, Leader, Field Marshall, Mobilizer
The Commandant of the World

Overview: You have indicated that you prefer Extraversion, iNtuition, Thinking, and Judging as your favorite ways of dealing with the world around you. By selecting those preferences, you join about 5% of the world's population who share the same personality type.

Other High Performers who share your type include: General Douglas MacArthur, Eleanor Roosevelt, LTC Ollie North, Lou Gerstner, Defense Secretary Donald Rumsfeld, conservative talk show host Rush Limbaugh, and Frank Lloyd Wright.

Snapshot: You act clearly and objectively on the basis of ideas that you consider to be logically and conceptually valid. You pride yourself on your clarity of thought and your ability to organize others and their ideas for the successful accomplishment of large tasks.

Leadership Style: Yours is one of the four types to rise most naturally to the leadership of large and complex organizations. In Fortune 500 Companies, your type comprises 20 % of presidents and CEO's, 11.2 % of senior and executive vice presidents, and 11.9 % of middle managers. If there is one type that is the natural born leader, it is the ENTJ. You have a knack for bringing together large and complex projects and dealing with them with strategic insight. You will have a vision and involve others in achieving it. Action and results surround your activities. You will work tirelessly, logically, and decisively to achieve anything you can be sure is conceptually valid.

How many of these traits apply to you?

__ You enjoy developing well-conceived grand plans

__ Complex problems interest and excite you

__ You can be tough and direct when you are in charge

__ You cannot, not lead, even when, positionally, you are not the one in charge

__ Your style is energetic and action oriented

__ Broad goals and visions are all you need to take a project to successful completion

__ When people speak to you they will get an answer or a decision. There is nothing wishy-washy about your responses

__ You prefer the long view to the immediate consequence

__ If someone wishes to persuade you they are correct and you are wrong, they should bring well-seasoned logic, not a deluge of data

__ You take charge quickly and effectively and lay out an approach for the organization to follow

Words to Live By: strategic, tough, decisive, objective, fair, planful, theoretical, straightforward, challenging, controlled, critical, logical, and dynamic.

Jobs and Careers That Attract Your Type: Military officer, executive, sales manager, consulting (business, management, education), account manager, engineer (chemical, environmental), talk show host, surgeon (cardiology), court room lawyer, program designer, stock broker, plant manager, economic advisor, international finance, management and sales trainer, labor relations, psychiatrist, intellectual property attorney, professor, marketing executive, logistics manager, and telecommunications.

Words You Use to Describe Yourself:_____

Extended Profile: If there is one type that is the born natural leader, it is yours. You probably find it very hard not taking charge, even when it is inappropriate. Others naturally look to you for leadership because of your remarkable abilities and forthright style. Yours is the type, which cannot not lead.

Quite frankly, you enjoy being in charge. Being the commander, the business director, the principal, or the orchestra conductor, appeals to you a lot more than being the executive officer, the human resources vice president, the teacher, or the second fiddle. You have the right stuff to be a tough-minded executive, and you are anxious to prove yourself.

The real virtue of being in charge is that you get to plan the show. Setting the vision and establishing the right tasks to accomplish the mission and aligning the right people for the tasks at hand strike you as being the stuff of leadership. You would much rather be called a leader than a manager. Being a manager strikes you as a bit beneath your abilities.

When you place other people at positions of leadership in your organization, you expect them to perform. If they cannot, or worse will not, you have no trouble removing them before they hurt the whole production. You are not one to pay people just for showing up. You expect high performance from others because that's all you know how to do. You set incredibly high standards for yourself and expect the same from others. If you are in an academic environment, you will challenge your teachers and professors on a daily basis. Once you find a chink in someone's armor, it is only a matter of time before you thrust in the lance.

The very power of your personality and presence sometimes hinders your ability to perform effectively, because others are often reluctant to level with you. This reluctance frustrates you because you encourage openness and candor; when you have been told in the past that people are afraid of you, you just do not understand. All persons with the letters "N" and "T" as their middle two letters face your dilemma to some degree. You learn by argument and debate. Someone will make a statement in a staff meeting or public town meeting, and you will challenge her or him back. You are not attacking the person; you are trying to refine your ideas so you can learn. Other types hear that challenge as an attack. "Wow, were you there when Johnson jumped all over Andrews, yesterday?"

You are a natural born critic. That title comes with your extraverted Thinking judgment. Asking "why?" strikes you as the appropriate question anytime someone makes an unsubstantiated claim or request for a change in budget. Others hear that as criticism. The truth is that you are a harsher critic of yourself. No matter how successful you are or how high you rise, you know you can do better, and behind closed doors or in conversation with an executive coach or trusted friend, you confess that you often see yourself as a failure—a failure who has risen higher than 99% of the population!

When you are confronted with a problem that seems insurmountable to most, you are energized. Others have rarely been able to stay up with you; your energy overwhelms them. Take this behavior to your home, and you can see how tough you can come across as a parent and even a mate. You expect to be in charge there as well.

When your child brings home a report card with five A's and a B, you know what the evening conversation is going to be about. Too often you neglect to praise her for the A's before you begin the "grilling" about the B. Your high expectations for yourself flow over to your children. Because you are someone who believes in living a disciplined life, there are clear rules around the house that all are expected to obey. When someone violates one of the rules, all it usually takes is the right look from you for them to know that they are in deep doo doo.

At work, people expect high results from you, and you rarely let them down. You work harder and longer than most and often can be found in your office after 6 PM. Go home!

Type and Age: Although you have elected just four preferences as your "type," life is an ongoing experience of learning how to use all eight preferences at the appropriate time, for the appropriate task. You will develop different preferences at specific, predictable times in your life.

For your type, the flow is as follows:
  Dominant—extraverted Thinking (ages 8-15)
  Auxiliary—introverted iNtuition (ages 16-30)
  Tertiary—extraverted Sensing (ages 31-40)
  Inferior—introverted Feeling (ages 41-55)

What we refer to as your Dominant function, is Thinking judgment, which you express externally. When you speak, we will hear decisions and get answers. There is nothing uncertain in your proclamations. You probably developed this preference first, between the ages 8-15. In arriving at your decisions, you have used your Auxiliary function, which is iNtuition. This function is expressed in the internal world; hence, you introvert it. You prefer quiet, alone time to reflect on the ideas, possibilities, theories, and models upon which you have made your decision. This function was likely developed between the ages of 16-30.

Hence, by the end of college or beginning of your early professional years, the Thinking–iNtuitive ground floor to your personality has been laid. The middle two letters of your personality type become the team of preferences that you will trust the most into the beginning of midlife.

About the age of 31, one of your non-preferences asks to be dealt with. We call it your Tertiary function. For your type, it is Sensing, which you extravert. When you begin considering data and factual information, you will tend to do it publicly, in the external world. Others may even be surprised that you are reflecting on such concerns, but they will begin to be important to you during this period. From the ages of 31 to about 40 you will develop the interest and the capacity to deal with the data. You may in fact start demanding more and more data from others to assist you in your deciding. Your type does not change, but you learn how to use this non-preference when required. Your last preference to be developed we call the Inferior function. For you, it is Feeling judgment, which you introvert. During the ages of 41-55 you will become more interested in thinking about the impact of your decisions on others; considerations which, heretofore, may have seemed extraneous, if not irrelevant, to you. When you use this function, you will do it in the internal world; hence, you introvert it.

Type, then, is far more than just 4 letters on a report form. If all goes well, and it rarely does, by late midlife, you will have developed the capacity to use each of the 8 preferences when needed, with some degree of sophistication. We call this process the full development of type.

Type Under Stress: Under heavy stress, you may show irrational anger at those closest to you. Normally, when using your dominant function, which is extraverted Thinking, you take charge in an impressive, rational way.

You chart clear paths to success and solve problems with verve. When you suddenly get trapped using your inferior function, which is introverted Feeling, everything changes. Your consistency and levelheaded approach turn to flaky and sometimes shaky performance. You may feel victimized, used, and persecuted. When you see others getting important assignments, you may feel yourself being passed by and ignored. You begin to lose confidence in yourself and make decisions which you will regret in the light of day. You may have emotional outbursts and react emotionally. Eventually, you may withdraw and fret over the problems rather than try to solve them. It is not unusual at these times for you to get a fierce headache, sinus attack, or severe backache.

Your Type and Ethics: Your approach to deciding what ethical behavior encompasses often surprises others. Values are incredibly important to you, and you often make that fact clear to others who live and work with you; however, values mean something altogether different to you than to other types. The persons involved or the rules that are broken are mostly irrelevant to you. What is important is the principle at stake, beneath the rules. In fact, you may be willing to break any rule or law that exists, as long as there is a clearer principle at stake behind the rule. Indeed, you may see the rules as merely arbitrary impediments to ethical behavior. You are willing to challenge them just as you would challenge any other arbitrary system. Once the principle at stake is clear, so is your necessary action. With ethics, as with most things in this life, you will seem antiauthoritarian and self-willed. For you, that is just fine.

Other ENTJ's That You Know_____